HANGED *AT*
LIVERPOOL

STEVE FIELDING

The History Press

Aerial photograph of Walton Gaol in the 1920s. (*Liverpool County Record Office*)

First published 2008

The History Press Ltd
The Mill, Brimscombe Port
Stroud, Gloucestershire, GL5 2QG
www.thehistorypress.co.uk

Reprinted 2010

British Library Cataloguing in Publication Data.
A catalogue record for this book is available from the British Library.

ISBN 978 0 7509 4751 0

Typesetting and origination by The History Press Ltd.
Printed in Great Britain

CONTENTS

MEMORANDUM OF INSTRUCTIONS FOR CARRYING OUT AN EXECUTION

1.   The trap doors shall be stained a dark colour and their outer edges shall be defined by a white line three inches broad painted round the edge of the pit outside the traps.

2.   (a) A week before an execution the apparatus for the execution shall be tested in the following manner under the supervision of the Works Officer, the Governor being present:-

The working of the scaffold will first be tested without any weight. Then a bag of dry sand of the same weight as the culprit will be attached to the rope and so adjusted as to allow the bag a drop equal to, or rather more than, that which the culprit should receive, so that the rope may be stretched with a force of not more than 1,000 foot-pounds. See Table of Drops. The working of the apparatus under these conditions will then be tested. The bag must be of the approved pattern, with a thick and well-padded neck, so as to prevent any injury to the rope and leather. Towelling will be supplied for padding the neck of the bag under the noose. As the gutta percha round the noose end of the execution ropes hardens in cold weather, care should be taken to have it warmed and manipulated immediately before the bag is tested.

(b) On the day before the execution the apparatus shall be tested again as above, the Governor, the Works Officer and the executioner being present. For the purpose of this test a note of the height and weight of the culprit should be obtained from the Medical Officer and handed to the executioner.

3.   After the completion of each test the scaffold and all the appliances will be locked up, and the key kept by the Governor or other responsible officer; but the bag of sand should remain suspended all the night preceding the execution so as to take the stretch out of the rope.

4.   The executioner and any persons appointed to assist in the operation should make themselves thoroughly acquainted with the working of the apparatus.

5.   In order to prevent accidents during the preliminary tests and procedure the lever will be fixed by a safety-pin, and the Works or other Prison Officer charged with the care of the apparatus prior to the execution will be responsible for seeing that the pin is properly in position both before and after the tests. The responsibility for withdrawing the pin at the execution will rest on the executioner.

6.   Death by hanging ought to result from dislocation of the neck. The length of the drop will be determined in accordance with the attached Table of Drops.

7.   The required length of drop is regulated as follows:-

(a) At the end of the rope which forms the noose the executioner should see that 13 inches from the centre of the ring are marked off by twine wrapped round the covering; this is to be a fixed quantity, which, with the stretching of this portion of the rope, and the lengthening of the neck and body of the culprit, will represent the average depth of the head and circumference of the neck after constriction.

(b) While the bag of sand is still suspended, the executioner will measure off from the painted line on the rope the required length of drop and will make a chalk mark on the rope at the end of this length. A piece of copper wire fastened to the chain will now be stretched down the rope till it reaches the chalk mark, and will be cut off there so that the cut end of the copper wire shall terminate at the upper end of the measured length of drop. The bag of sand will then be raised from the pit, and disconnected from the rope.

(The chain ......

Above & opposite: Memo on how to carry out an execution. (*Author's collection*)

The chain will now be so adjusted at the bracket that the lower end of the copper wire shall reach to the same level from the floor of the scaffold as the height of the prisoner. The known height of the prisoner can be readily measured on the scaffold by a graduated rule of six foot six inches long. When the chain has been raised to the proper height the cotter must be securely fixed through the bracket and chain. The executioner will now make a chalk mark on the floor of the scaffold, in a plumb line with the chain, where the prisoner should stand.

(c) These details will be attended to as soon as possible after 6 a.m. on the day of the execution so as to allow the rope time to regain a portion of its elasticity before the execution, and, if possible, the gutta percha on the rope should again be warmed.

8. The copper wire will now be detached, and after allowing sufficient amount of rope for the easy adjustment of the noose, the slack of the rope should be fastened to the chain above the level of the head of the culprit with a pack-thread. The pack-thread should be just strong enough to support the rope without breaking.

9. When all the preparations are completed the scaffold will remain in the charge of a responsible officer until the time fixed for the execution.

10. At the time fixed for the execution, the executioner will go to the pinioning room, which should be as close as practicable to the scaffold, and there apply the apparatus. When the culprit is pinioned and his neck is bared he will be at once conducted to the scaffold.

11. On reaching the scaffold the procedure will be as follows:-

   (a) The executioner will:-

      (i) Place the culprit exactly under the part of the beam to which the rope is attached.

      (ii) Put the white linen cap on the culprit.

      (iii) Put on the rope round the neck quite tightly (with the cap between the rope and the neck), the metal eye being directed forwards, and placed in front of the angle of the lower jaw, so that with the constriction of the neck it may come underneath the chin. The noose should be kept tight by means of a stiff leather washer, or an india rubber washer, or a wedge.

   (b) While the executioner is carrying out the procedure in paragraph (a) the assistant executioner will:-

      (i) Strap the culprit's legs tightly.

      (ii) Step back beyond the white safety line so as to be well clear of the trap doors.

      (iii) Give an agreed visual signal to the executioner to show that he is clear.

   (c) On receipt of the signal from his assistant the executioner will:-

      (i) Withdraw the safety pin.

      (ii) Pull the lever which lets down the trap doors.

12. The body will ~~THEN~~ be carefully raised from the pit ~~as soon as~~ *PROVIDED* the Medical Officer declares life to be extinct. Then the body will be detached from the rope and removed to the place set aside for the Coroner's inspection, a careful record having first been made and given to the Medical Officer of both the initial and final drops. The rope will be removed from the neck, and also the straps from the body. In laying out the body for the inquest the head will be raised three inches by placing a small piece of wood under it.

WILL HANG FOR A MINIMUM OF 45 MINUTES, AND

ABOUT THE AUTHOR

S teve Fielding was born in Bolton, Lancashire in the 1960s. He attended Bolton County Grammar School and served an apprenticeship as an engineer before embarking on a career as a professional musician. After many years recording and touring, both in Great Britain and Europe, he began writing in 1993 and had his first book published a year later. He is the author of over a dozen books on the subject of true crime, and in particular hangmen and executions.

Hanged at Liverpool is the third in a series and follows *Hanged at Durham* and *Hanged at Pentonville* (both Sutton Publishing). He compiled the first complete study of modern-day executions, *The Hangman's Record 1868–1964*, and, as well as writing a number of regional murder casebooks, is also the author of two titles on executioners: *Pierrepoint: A Family of Executioners* and *The Executioner's Bible – Hangmen of the 20th Century*. He is a regular contributor to magazines including the *Criminologist*, *Master Detective* and *True Crime*, and is Historical Consultant for the Discovery Channel series *The Executioners*, and *Executioner: Pierrepoint* for the Crime & Investigation channel. Beside writing, he teaches maths and English at a local college.

Forthcoming titles in the series include:

Hanged at Manchester
Hanged at Leeds
Hanged at Birmingham
Hanged at Wandsworths
Hanged at Durham
Hanged at Pentonville

ACKNOWLEDGEMENTS

I would like to thank the following people for help with this book. Firstly to Lisa Moore for her help in every stage of the production, but mainly with the photographs and proofreading. I offer my sincere thanks to both Tim Leech, who once again allowed me access to his archives, and to Matthew Spicer, who likewise was willing to share information along with rare documents, photos and illustrations from his own collection. I would also like to thank Janet Buckingham for her help in inputting much of the original data and to Gillian Papaioannou who proofread and edited early drafts of the text. Thanks also to Stewart McLaughlin who helped with information and papers relating to HMP Liverpool.

RESEARCH MATERIALS & SOURCES

As with my other books in this series and with the subject of capital punishment and executions in general, a great number of people have helped with information, anecdotes and photographs. I remain indebted to the help with rare photographs and material given to me by the late Syd Dernley (assistant executioner) and former prison officer, the late Frank McKue.

Research on cases, which would eventually form this book, began many years ago, with extra information added to my records as and when it has become available. In most instances, contemporary local and national newspapers have supplied the basic information, which has been supplemented by material found in PCOM, HO and ASSI files held at the National Record Office at Kew. I also had access to the Home Office Capital Case File 1901-1948, along with personal information, papers, diaries, photographs etc. from a number of those directly involved in some of the cases.

Space doesn't permit a full bibliography of books and websites accessed while researching this project. I have tried to locate the copyright owners of all images used in this book, but a number of them were untraceable, in particular those sourced from the National Archives. I apologise if I have inadvertently infringed any existing copyright.

INTRODUCTION

Work began on a new gaol in Liverpool early in 1850. Situated on Hornby Road, Walton, and covering nearly 20 acres, it took almost five years to complete, at a cost of almost £3,500, and a company named Furness & Co was tasked with carrying out work. Architects Charles Pierce and John Weightman based the plans on the radial or panopticon design that had proved a big success in several newly-built American penitentiaries and more recently at London's Pentonville Prison. This new design allowed a warder a panoramic view of all the prison wings from a central area, and prisoners now had there own 'separate' cells with improved lighting and sanitation facilities.

At the time of completion, Walton was the most modern prison in the country and had been commissioned to replace the archaic New Borough Gaol. Situated close to the dockside, the old gaol had, at one time, been a holding pen for slaves bound for the West Indies and the Americas and had also held so many French prisoners of war during the Napoleonic Wars, it became known locally as the French Gaol.

Liverpool became an Assize town in 1835. Prior to this, criminals tried for crimes in the city were taken to either Chester or Lancaster for trial and execution. The first execution in Liverpool took place in August 1835, in public, outside the walls of Kirkdale House of Correction. Despite the construction of the more modern Walton Gaol, Kirkdale was still the main prison serving Liverpool, and in the latter years of the nineteenth century, it gradually became the main centre of execution for the county of Lancashire. All executions took place outside the prison walls and in some instances, crowds of up to 50,000 would congregate to witness the gruesome spectacle. (*See* Appendix I for a complete list of public executions at Kirkdale.)

The imposing courtrooms at St George's Hall were opened in the 1854, and it was here, throughout the nineteenth and twentieth centuries, that numerous infamous trials were held, many that filled the pages of the newspapers across the whole country. It was also here, where the majority of those hanged at Liverpool were sentenced to death.

Walton Gaol had originally been conceived to hold one thousand inmates and took both male and female prisoners. With executions of male prisoners still carried out at Kirkdale, following the Private Executions Act of 1868, it was decided that females sentenced to death would henceforth be hanged at Walton. Elizabeth Berry was the first to go to the gallows here (*see* chapter 1) and Mrs Berry's terror as she heard the prison carpenters erecting the scaffold was also shared by the next inmate in the new condemned cell at the gaol.

In 1889, American born Florence Maybrick, convicted of the murder of her husband by poisoning him with arsenic, came within days of being included in the list of those hanged at Liverpool, before the intervention of the American authorities persuaded Queen Victoria to sanction a pardon. The Maybrick case returned to the headlines in the 1990s when a diary and papers found beneath the floorboards in a renovated house in Liverpool seemed to suggest that James Maybrick, the victim in the case, had in fact been the notorious London murderer Jack the Ripper. Maybrick's untimely death had coincided with a halt to the reign of terror. Whether this is true or the diaries are a forgery is still the subject of debate.

In 1890, inmates from Kirkdale were transferred to Walton, being marched under armed escort from prison to prison, and although all prisoners were now sent to Walton to serve their sentences, executions continued at Kirkdale until August of the following year. Kirkdale closed completely in 1892 and was later demolished; a park now stands on the spot where the gaol once was. (A list of latter day executions at Kirkdale can be found in Appendix II.)

The first gallows constructed at Walton was situated in the coach house in the grounds of the prison. Following the passing of sentence of death on Mrs Berry, a dozen inmates were hurriedly detailed to dig a large pit, which was then bricked up and the trapdoor and beam assembly constructed on top. It was seemingly believed that the prisoner would not be hanged, or at least not hanged at Walton, and as a result no effort had been made to construct a scaffold until she was brought to the prison pending execution.

By the turn of the twentieth century, Liverpool was one of busiest centres of execution in the country, dealing with condemned prisoners from all parts of the north-west. In the years leading up to the First World War, there were several nearby prisons that housed a gallows: both Knutsford and Lancaster played host to the hangmen, as, of course, did Manchester's Strangeways Prison. When Knutsford was closed down and Lancaster downgraded during the First World War, all subsequent convicted criminals went either to Liverpool or Manchester for execution. Likewise, when Stafford Gaol was similarly requisitioned as a military prison and detention centre in 1916, a number of condemned criminals from Staffordshire also found themselves in the condemned cell at Walton.

In line with Home Office recommendations, work began early in 1929 on modernising the execution suite, which was to now be situated on landing two, I wing, where it remained in regular use until abolition.

Like other gaols around the country, Walton did not retain its own executioner. The under-sheriffs of the county in which the condemned prisoner had been sentenced retained a copy of the short Home Office list of hangmen and assistants and selected an executioner from that, with the prison governor being responsible for recruiting the assistant executioner. Initially the hangman had worked alone but by the turn of the century it became common, and then eventually a rule, to employ an assistant executioner.

The first hangman to officiate at Walton was former Bradford policeman, James Berry. Berry had been an executioner since 1884 and had been a frequent visitor to the city, officiating at Kirkdale on a number of occasions, and where he came into contact with Medical Officer Dr James Barr. The relationship between these two men was to become strained in August 1891 when they failed to agree on the correct drop for a man to be hanged for a brutal child murder. Berry wanted to give the prisoner a drop of under 5ft; Dr Barr insisted nearer 7ft was suitable. When the prisoner dropped to his death on the following morning, there was a horrendous squelch from the pit instead of a thud and the prisoner was almost decapitated, with blood squirting everywhere. On the following day Berry tendered his resignation and blamed the doctor's interference in this execution as his reason for doing so.

James Billington succeeded Berry, and even though Billington had been carrying out executions on his own since 1884, he was still sent to Kirkdale to receive further instruction in carrying out executions from Dr Barr. Barr had given evidence at the Aberdare Report in 1886, which had been set up following a number of botched executions by James Berry. Following the retirement of Berry, the prison authorities began to take steps to make sure any future hangmen engaged or recruited to the list were suitable, both mentally and physically.

Billington carried out eight executions at Walton, often assisted in the later engagements by one of his sons. At the execution of Winstanley in December 1895, Billington was to have been assisted by Thomas Scott, a Huddersfield-born rope maker, who had acted as his assistant on a number of occasions across the country, and who had even carried out a number of jobs himself as a chief executioner. On arriving at Lime Street in good time, Scott decided to while away the afternoon in the company of a lady of dubious virtue. Scott and his companion, Winifred Webb, spent several hours together and their parting was the subject of a quarrel over a small matter of money.

Hangman James Berry, the first
executioner to officiate at Walton
Gaol. (*Author's collection*)

James Billington carried out eight
executions at Walton until the
turn of the twentieth century.
(*T.J. Leech Archive*)

Scott discovered he had been robbed of a pair of spectacles along with £2 9s 6d and contacted the police, only for the woman to counter this by saying he had given her the money as payment for her company. By the time the matter was resolved, Scott was too late to attend the prison and was unable to assist at the execution, leaving Billington to go to work alone.

Following James Billington's death in December 1901, his son William officiated at the execution of John Harrison. The engagement had already been in his father's diary, but responsibility was passed to William who carried out the execution assisted by his elder brother, Thomas. When William was next engaged at Walton five months later, Thomas had also passed away and William's assistant on this occasion was his younger brother, John.

Henry Pierrepoint assisted William Billington on two executions at the gaol and during his reign as a chief executioner, he also officiated twice at Liverpool. His assistant on both occasions was his elder brother, Thomas. Thomas Pierrepoint also worked as an assistant to John Ellis in 1911 but it would be over fifteen years before he was next on duty at Walton Gaol.

John Ellis carried out twelve executions in thirteen years, including two doubles. Following his retirement in 1924, William Willis, who was living in Manchester, succeeded Ellis, but Willis was to officiate just twice at Liverpool before being struck off the Home Office list of hangmen. This short list was periodically updated, and it was the failure to use an up-to-date list that caused an unfortunate situation in 1926 when William Willis was engaged to execute James Leah.

Unbeknown to the hangman, he had been struck off the list following indiscretions at a previous execution at Pentonville a few months earlier, and when Willis received the letter he wrote accepting the engagement, only to receive a further letter withdrawing the offer of the job and telling the shocked hangman that he had been sacked. The engagement was then offered to, and accepted by Thomas Pierrepoint. Willis wrote several times to the Home Office asking for an explanation and begging for his job back but it was not to be.

Almost twelve months later when William Robertson was sentenced to death, Willis was contacted asking if he was free to officiate. Believing he must have served some suspension which had now been lifted, Willis wrote at once stating that he was available, but as before, he received a further letter several days later saying the offer had to be withdrawn, as he was no longer on the official list of executioners. The Home Office later wrote to the under-sheriff, haughtily reminding him that it was his responsibility to use an up-to-date list of hangmen when engaging an executioner and not one that was out of date.

Thomas Pierrepoint was the longest serving hangman at the gaol, executing thirteen men in a career that lasted almost forty years. Following adverse reports into his conduct during the early years of the Second World War, Tom Pierrepoint was subjected to a Home Office investigation, and an official report regarding the execution of Roberts at Walton in 1943 recorded that the aged hangman (he was 73 at the time and walking with a stick) deemed speed to be the basic requisite of an executioner's capabilities. The memo noted that Pierrepoint was so swift in darting to the lever once the noose was in place, that assistant Harry Kirk barely had time to get clear of the trapdoors.

By this time Tom's nephew and Henry Pierrepoint's son, Albert Pierrepoint, was also an established executioner. Ten years earlier, in 1933, Albert had assisted his uncle at the execution of Richard Hetherington. It was Albert's first bona-fide engagement as an assistant in a British prison, and over twenty years later, Pierrepoint's career ended with an execution at Walton when he resigned a few months after hanging Norman Green.

Curiously, Manchester-born hangman Steve Wade, a rival to Albert Pierrepoint as a chief executioner in the post-war years, carried out just two senior executions at Walton, and on both occasions, the prisoners had been convicted for crimes that took place in Staffordshire.

Liverpool holds a place in the annals of criminal history as the scene of one of the last two executions to take place in Great Britain, when Robert Leslie 'Jock' Stewart hanged Peter Allen at the same moment that Allen's partner-in-crime was hanged at Manchester.

Left: Bomb-damaged wing
at Walton, 1942. (*Liverpool
County Record Office*)

Below: Modern-day photograph
of HMP Liverpool. (*Author's
collection*)

Walton had become an exclusively male prison in 1933. In 1941, parts of the prison were subject to damage from German bombs. Over twenty prisoners were killed in the raids, which demolished two of the eight wings of the gaol. In 1980 the prison was extended and extra cells were added, making its capacity of over 1,350 one of the largest in the country. Now covering an area of over 22 acres, it was officially renamed HMP Liverpool and continues to be in use as a prison to this day.

Here within its walls, over a period spanning seventy-seven years between 1887 and 1964, a total of sixty men and two women were to pay the ultimate penalty. This book looks in detail at the sixty cases in which the killers were all *Hanged at Liverpool*.

Steve Fielding, 2008
www.stevefielding.com

1

'THE WORST SPECIES OF WOMANKIND'

Elizabeth Berry, 14 March 1887

On Saturday morning, New Year's Day 1887, nurse Elizabeth Berry, a 31-year-old widow, was on duty at the Oldham Infirmary Workhouse. For the last three days her daughter, 11-year-old Edith Annie, had been staying with her at the hospital and that morning after Berry had prepared a pan of sago, her daughter ate a bowlful and became violently sick.

An hour later, with her daughter still vomiting, she asked one of the doctors to examine Edith and the child was prescribed a medicine, containing a mixture of iron and quinine. At lunchtime on the following day, the doctor examined Edith again and thought that she was over the worst, and would make a full recovery. Berry, however, told him that the girl was still being sick and showed him a towel stained with blood and vomit, which had a strange acid smell. The doctor asked for the key to the medicine cupboard so he could prepare a bicarbonate mixture. Mrs Berry had the only key to this cabinet and when the doctor opened it, he noticed a bottle of creosote on one of the shelves.

That night the child was again taken ill and this time the doctor noticed faint red blisters around her mouth. He consulted another doctor at the adjacent infirmary and the two decided that the girl must have taken a corrosive poison. She was given further medication, which she immediately vomited. The child began to weaken rapidly, and by the following day there was hardly any sign of a pulse and the doctors feared the worst.

Edith Berry died in the early hours of Thursday morning and because the cause of death was suspicious, an autopsy was ordered before a death certificate could be issued. With the help of a surgeon from Manchester Hospital, an autopsy was carried out which revealed the cause of death as by an acidic, caustic poison, similar in colour to creosote. Remembering the bottle he had seen in the medicine cabinet, the doctor informed the police and later that day, Mrs Berry was arrested for the murder of her daughter.

Her trial before Mr Justice Hawkins at Liverpool Assizes began on 21 February, and over the next four days, a number of medical experts all testified that the cause of death was corrosive poison.

The prosecution also suggested a motive claiming that in April 1886, Mrs Berry had received a sum of one £100 from an assurance society following the sudden death of her mother. It was found that later that year Mrs Berry tried to insure both herself and her daughter for £100 with the money to go to the survivor, after one or the other had died. Although she had not paid the full premiums, she had made a number of payments and would have expected the insurance to be settled. She was never to get a chance to make the claim.

The prosecution also suspected that she had poisoned her mother the previous year and five years before, had disposed of her husband in a similar fashion. In 1883, her son had also died suddenly and following this loss she had come to an arrangement with her sister-in-law for the

Above left: Mrs Elizabeth Berry, the first person hanged at Walton. (*T.J. Leech Archive*)

Above right: Eleven-year-old Edith Berry, poisoned by her mother. (*T.J. Leech Archive*)

Left: The execution of Mrs Berry made headlines across the country. (*T.J. Leech Archive*)

THE

OLDHAM

POISONING CASE.

EXECUTION

OF

MRS. BERRY.

[SPECIAL TELEGRAMS]

[FIRST REPORT.]

The execution of Mrs. Berry, for the murder of her daughter Edith Annie, by poisoning, took place at Walton Gaol this morning, at eight o'clock. James Berry, of Bradford, who was the executioner, arrived at the gaol at five o'clock on Saturday afternoon, and inspected the arrangements, which he found were most complete and satisfactory. He tested the trap, which worked all right, and then decided to allow a drop of 4 feet 6 inches. The scene on the scaffold was distressing, upkeep of young Edith. Elizabeth was earning a yearly wage of £25, and she paid almost half of her salary to her sister-in-law for the child's upkeep. With Edith's sudden death, this payment ceased and helped support the prosecution's claims that it was murder for greed and financial gain. The jury agreed and took just ten minutes to find her guilty as charged.

The execution date was fixed for Monday 14 March 1887 and Yorkshire hangman James Berry was engaged. On his arrival at the gaol, the governor met him with a smile. 'I did not know you were going to hang an old flame, Mr Berry.' he told the startled hangman. Berry insisted that he wasn't and thought this was due to the confusion of their sharing the same surname.

'Oh no, she tells me she knows you very well' the governor said, 'you had better go and have a look at her tonight. I will make the necessary arrangements.'

When Berry spied her in her cell, he recognised the woman as someone he had met in the past. They had been introduced at a policeman's ball in Manchester, and after sharing refreshments and several dances, he discovered they were travelling home in the same direction, and invited her to join him in his cab. They parted with a friendly kiss when she alighted his train at Oldham railway station.

As there had not been an execution at Walton before, the prison did not have a designated condemned cell and Mrs Berry was housed in the female debtors' wing, which was close to where the gallows was to be situated. She complained to the warders that she could hear the prison carpenters assembling the gallows in the adjacent coach house, and as a result, she was moved to a cell in another wing of the prison. With preparation for the scaffold completed, she was brought back to her original cell and it was here where Berry spoke to her on the night before her execution. When the hangman entered the cell she looked up and smiled.

The Thompson Weekly News superimposed the hangman and his victim on the front gate of Walton when serialising James Berry's memoirs. (*T.J. Leech Archive*)

'Good evening Mrs Berry,' he said kindly.

'You've no doubt heard a lot of dreadful things about me, but it isn't all true what people say,' she told him, adding, 'you need not be a bit afraid of me, Mr Berry. You don't suppose I'd want to give you any trouble, do you?'

'I hope you won't give me any trouble,' Berry replied, 'I shall not prolong your life a single minute. Have you made your peace with God?'

As he left the cell, Berry was not convinced the prisoner would be true to her word and told one of the guards rather harshly: 'That woman is one of the biggest cowards in the world.'

Snow was falling heavily on the morning of the execution, but despite this, the street outside the gaol was described in the local newspaper as being 'black with people,' eager to witness the black flag that signified an execution had been carried out, hoisted on the flagpole at Walton.

In company of the governor and prison doctor, Berry entered the cell at a minute before 8 a.m. 'Is there anything I can do for you before you leave the condemned cell?' Berry asked.

The prisoner shivered, slunk back into her chair and shook her head. With her arms pinioned, the governor led the way as the procession formed. The distance from the cell to the scaffold was around 60yd, and sand had been thrown liberally along the ground to prevent anyone slipping. Mrs Berry walked firmly until she turned the angle of the building and saw the gallows' shed. At that, a cry of sheer terror left her lips.

'Oh, dear!' she wailed loudly, and slumped back as if in a faint. Berry rushed forward and steadied her. 'Let me go, Mr. Berry,' she begged, 'let me go, and I will go bravely.'

Supported by two warders, she struggled to complete the final few yards until she reached the scaffold. 'God forbid!' she cried before collapsing into a faint. Warders held her beneath the beam as Berry completed his preparations and pulled the lever.

No sooner had the trapdoors crashed open, one of the wardresses approached the hangman. 'There goes one of the coldest-blooded murderers. She must be the worst species of womankind to carry out the deeds she has carried out' she spat bitterly.

2
'FOR A GOOD CAUSE'

Patrick Gibbons, 17 August 1892

Following his discharge from the Lancashire Fusiliers in the summer of 1892, 33-year-old private Patrick Gibbons moved back to live with his parents on Water Street, Heyside, a small village on the outskirts of Oldham.

The homecoming was not a happy one and the family soon began to argue and fight almost daily. The root of the trouble was that both parents and son regularly drank to excess and this culminated in a drinking binge that was to end in tragedy.

By the morning of Saturday 9 July, Gibbons and his parents had spent the last three days in an almost permanent drunken stupor, and throughout that time, neighbours had heard constant raised voices, along with shouts and threats being made. Gibbons left the house before noon and went to a local pub where he consumed several drinks before returning home, and was seen by neighbours staggering along the street and clearly drunk.

His father was out at the time, leaving Patrick Gibbons' 62-year-old mother Bridget alone in the house, sleeping off her hangover. Returning home, Gibbons picked up his razor, crept into his mother's bedroom and as she slept he cut her throat. He then put the razor down and went to the house next door, asking a neighbour to come to their house.

'Mrs Russell, go and look at my mother – I have done it,' he told her. Asked what he had done, he replied that he had cut her throat. 'Go and see for yourself' he told her, before sitting down in a chair and waiting for her to come back. Mrs Russell entered the house, climbed the stairs and found Bridget Gibbons lying face down in a pool of blood. The body was still warm. The police were summoned and when Inspector Ormrod arrived and placed Gibbons under arrest, he said he had done it 'for a good cause' but did not elaborate.

At his trial before Mr Justice Denman at Liverpool Assizes on Friday 29 July, his defence was based on the fact that he had been too drunk to be aware of what he was doing. The prosecution countered this by saying that the statement he had made to the arresting officer, that he had killed her 'for a good cause' suggested that he did know what he was doing and although the motive was not made clear, there was, nonetheless, a motive.

Gibbons had shown great penitence following conviction and after a farewell interview with his father on the Tuesday afternoon, he admitted that he was responsible for the crime but had no recollection of it due to drink.

3

A POSITIVE IDENTIFICATION

Cross Duckworth, 3 January 1893

The man leaning on the fence seemed to be watching the two young girls intently. They were driving a number of cows into Witton Park, Blackburn, and the way he was staring unnerved them to the extent they were glad when they passed him by without incident and exited the park farther along at the opposite side.

On Tuesday 8 November 1892, shortly before 1 p.m., youngsters Martha Hindle and Harry Riding were making their way back to school along on a rough path that bordered Witton Park. Up ahead they saw a man behaving suspiciously and as they approached, he dropped a bundle to the ground and fled. Getting closer, they discovered the body of a young girl lying face down in a puddle of mud. They also saw the man flee from the park where he disappeared in the direction of Spring Lane. They rushed to tell a neighbour and Mrs Ellen Ormerod hurried to the scene and discovered that although the child was still warm, she was dead.

Detectives arrived at the park and as they searched for clues, the police surgeon, Dr James Wheatley examined the body, which had been identified as 8-year-old Alice Barnes, the daughter of a farmer at nearby Redlam. Wheatley found that Alice had suffered a severe head

THE BLACKBURN TRAGEDY.

TRIAL AT THE LIVERPOOL ASSIZES.

THE CASE FOR THE PROSECUTION.

In the Crown Court of the Liverpool Assizeszes
>efore Mr. Justice Grantham, yesterday, Crosros;
Juckworth (32), brass finisher, was charged with itl
he willful murder of Alice Barns on the 8t|8t|
Novembnber, at Witto near Blackburn. DrDr
J'Feeleyley and Mr. J. Rkill conducted the casas
or the ps prosecution, and the prison was defendede
by Mr. r. M'Keand. The court warowded, an an
during g the hearing of the evidence prisonone
was proovided with a seat. When forlly chargerge
the prisoner in full voice pleaded at guilty.

Dr. O'Feeley, in opening the case for the prosros
cution, said that the prisoner was born in Blaclac!

Newspaper cutting of the Blackburn murder. (*T.J. Leech Archive*)

wound and had cuts on her hands and arms, but the cause of death was suffocation, caused by having a man's red pocket handkerchief forced into her mouth, presumably to prevent her from screaming. From the position of her clothes, it seemed that the killer had attempted to rape the young girl but he had clearly been disturbed and taken flight before he could commit the foul deed.

Officers decided to enlist the help of an amateur detective from Bromley Cross, Bolton, complete with two bloodhounds, but by the time they arrived at the scene, the trail had gone cold. Also, a large crowd had since gathered and the hounds had no chance of picking up the killer's scent. Detectives did, however, find the imprints of heavy hobnailed boots and had casts made of them.

Witnesses were able to give police a good description of the man seen loitering in the vicinity of the park shortly before the murder and from the children who had seen him run away. He was described as being aged around 35–40 years of age, 5ft 6in tall, slender with a dark moustache and wearing fustian trousers and vest, a black coat and billycock hat and a spotted muffler.

Over the next twenty-four hours, several men who roughly fitted the description were taken into custody on suspicion of the crime, but all were able to prove their innocence and were subsequently released. Another who fitted the description was 32-year-old Cross Duckworth, who lived with his wife and two young children on Primrose Street, Bower House Fold, in the Mill Hill area, not far from Witton Park. Duckworth was a former soldier who had recently lost his job as a brass dresser at a local mill, and had been spending most of his days getting drunk and loitering on street corners. He became an immediate suspect when he greeted the detectives who knocked on his door with the words: 'Have you come to see me about the murder?' Officers searched his house and uncovered a pair of muddy hobnail boots and two handkerchiefs similar to the one used to gag the victim. The boots were found to be identical to the cast taken from beside the body and on the strength of this, he was arrested and charged with murder.

Cross Duckworth stood trial at Liverpool Assizes on Monday 12 December. His alibi for the day of the murder, that he had been delivering coal with his brother, had a number of gaps in it, particularly around 12.45 p.m. when it was thought that the murder had taken place. Duckworth claimed to have been drinking in the Unicorn public house at this time, but the landlord stated that he had left the pub at 12.40 p.m. saying that he was going home for lunch.

Witnesses called by the prosecution testified to the strength of the evidence matching the boots taken from Duckworth's house to the plaster cast made at the scene of the crime, in particular, the unusual pattern of the nails, which was identical.

Crucially, Duckworth was also identified as the man seen loitering at the fence by the two young girls shortly before Alice was killed, and also by the two children driving cattle, who had seen him drop the child to the ground and flee the scene.

Summing up, trial judge, Mr Justice Grantham, told the jury that the evidence of the plaster casts should not be relied on alone, nor should they neglect the positive identifications made by the children, just because of their ages. Retiring to consider their verdict, they took less that an hour to find him guilty as charged.

'I have nothing to say except that I am not guilty,' Duckworth declared, before sentence of death was passed on him.

From the condemned cell at Walton, he wrote to the Home Secretary, claiming the prosecution's case was based on flawed identification and that the police had fabricated the case against him. Reviewing the case papers, Home Secretary Herbert Asquith believed that the evidence presented in court was correct and based on positive identification, and he declined to interfere with the verdict of the court.

4

THE PRISONER IN THE ATTIC

Margaret Walber, 2 April 1894

Fifty-year-old French polisher John Walber lived with his wife Margaret, 53, and stepson John Murray at 6 Gildart Street, Liverpool. Theirs was a large house and the ground floor had been turned into a small grocery and provisions shop, while rooms on the upper floors were let out to a number of lodgers. By the autumn of 1893, they had been married for five years, and with both being addicted to drink, they lived together unhappily.

In the summer of 1876, Walber had lived with a woman named Anne Connolly. They had parted after just a matter of weeks and did not see each other again until seventeen years later in the spring of 1893, when Anne Connolly took lodgings in a house on Oakes Street, a few yards away from the Walbers' house. Once John Walber discovered his former lover was living close by, he renewed their acquaintance and made several visits to Oakes Street.

Margaret Walber was a very jealous woman and when word reached her that her husband had been visiting the house, she became enraged. She accused her husband of rekindling his romance with Anne Connolly, but he repeatedly denied the accusations. Still, rumours persisted and one afternoon in May, Margaret decided to find out for herself if they were true. Walber left the house saying that he was going for a drink, and as he walked off down the street, she crept out of the door and followed him. She watched him cross London Road, make his way down Oakes Street and enter a house. Convinced now of his infidelity, Margaret Walber stormed up to the front door, burst in and set about her husband with feet and fists, until anger sated, she walked out and slammed the door.

When John Walber returned home later they continued to quarrel until he finally collapsed in a drunken heap. When he awoke, he found the extent that his infidelity had enraged his wife. She had, with the help from her son, carried her husband into an attic bedroom where she chained him to a wall and kept the door locked with a padlock and chain.

For the next four months Walber never left the room; indeed, he never left the house alive. He was stripped of his clothes, which she hid in a cellar, and lodgers were told by Margaret that her husband was sick and needed rest.

On 16 November, Margaret Walber went to the bank and withdrew over £4. She then proceeded to get drunk and lodgers later heard sounds of a great disturbance coming from the attic. She then confessed to one of them that her son had beaten her husband to death, stolen the money she had drawn out and fled.

The police were called and found John Walber lying in a pool of blood on the attic floor. He had been lashed repeatedly with a chain and then battered to death with the heavy porcelain chamber pot. There were streaks of blood on all of the walls and on the bed and as a manhunt was set up for the missing son, detectives questioned Margaret Walber at the police station. They soon found discrepancies in her account of what had happened and when her clothes were examined, they were found to be bloodstained.

She maintained that her son was responsible for the murder and John Murray was traced to Dublin and brought back for questioning. He claimed that he had fled the scene after being given two sovereigns by his mother for his passage after he had witnessed her carry out the brutal murder of her husband.

Margaret Walber stood trial before Mr Justice Day at Liverpool Assizes on 14 March 1894. The trial lasted over a day but with the prosecution putting forward a strong case, it didn't take the jury long to bring in a guilty verdict.

Margaret was hanged on Easter Monday by James Billington, who gave her a drop of 6ft 7ins. As with previous executions carried out at Walton, the press were not admitted, although the governor told the coroner's inquest held later that afternoon that she had walked to the gallows with a steady step and that death was instant.

5

'FOR HER UNFAITHFULNESS'

John Langford, 22 May 1894

John Langford was a 41-year-old foreman baker who had seperated from his wife and had been left with custody of their three children. Since the break-up of his marriage four years earlier, he had been co-habiting with 28-year-old Elizabeth Stephen. She was also separated from her husband and had a young family, and all of them shared a house at 110 Cockerel Street, Walton Road, in the Kirkdale district of Liverpool.

Both had intemperate habits and throughout their time together, they quarrelled often, usually after they had been drinking, and because Langford had a very jealous nature and suspected her of having affairs while he was working through the night in a bakery.

On the morning of 3 April 1894, Langford finished the night shift and returned home to find the house empty. The previous day had been Easter Monday and Elizabeth had spent the afternoon and evening drinking and Langford suspected she was out with another man. Langford had also stopped off for a drink on the way home from work and was already drunk.

At shortly after noon he called into Cain's public house on the corner of Florence Street and Walton Lane and as he suspected, she was there, drinking with a group of friends, including a number of men. Without waiting for an explanation, Langford launched himself at her, punching her in the head. He was restrained by the landlord, Francis Lennon, and held firmly as the publican ordered Elizabeth and her friends out of the pub. Langford was detained for a few minutes until the landlord sensed they were clear away and then let him go.

Had Elizabeth chosen to go for more drinks, she may have avoided confrontation with the enraged Langford; instead, she headed home and it was as she was approaching the entry at the back of their home that he caught up with her. Langford grabbed her by the shoulder, spun her round and thrust the knife into her breast, mortally wounding her. As she lay slumped on the floor moaning pitifully and with blood oozing out on the pavement, he dropped to his knees declaring, 'We shall die together!' He then drew the knife across his own throat several times. The suicide attempt failed and with only slight injuries to his neck, Langford was taken into custody. He claimed he had attacked her 'for her unfaithfulness.'

Elizabeth Stephen died from her injuries in Stanley Hospital and at the beginning of May, Langford stood before Mr Justice Day charged with wilful murder. The prosecution said that he had been enraged because Elizabeth had pawned a number of items from their house and had then used the money to go out drinking with friends.

Langford's counsel pleaded that he was drunk at the time of the murder and that the charge should be one of manslaughter on account of her infidelity, which had led to her death. The judge refused to allow a plea of manslaughter and the jury took just a short time to return a guilty verdict, but with a strong recommendation to mercy.

Unlike previous executions at Walton, Langford's execution was the first to be witnessed by members of the press who later that day described in detail the moments leading up to the sentence being carried out. They wrote that Langford had risen early and had had an interview with the chaplain, the Reverend Morris, who had found the prisoner deeply contrite. As the hangman, James Billington, went to work in the timber-built execution shed erected in the prison grounds, securing the trapdoors and preparing the noose, Langford ate his last meal, the usual prison breakfast, and by the time he had finished his meal, the clock was approaching the fatal hour.

At a few minutes to eight, the governor, Dr Beamish, along with the under-sheriff of Lancashire, Mr Wilson of Preston, and several prison officials arrived at the corridor that led to the gallows. Langford was taken from his cell to a smaller room at the end of the corridor where the pinioning was to take place. Langford entered the room which was empty apart from a chair and a table on which rested the straps and hood belonging to the hangman. Langford winced as he noticed them and realised their sinister purpose, but he soon regained composure. Billington pinioned the prisoner on the stroke of eight as the doleful procession formed, and the chaplain, in a loud voice recited: 'I am the Resurrection and the Life.'

It was only a few paces from the corridor to the gallows and as Langford took his place on the trapdoors, his feet in line with a chalk mark Billington had made over the joint of the heavy doors, the hangman secured his ankles with a strap, placed a linen bag over his head and then positioned the noose. The chaplain continued the litany as Billington retired deftly to the side and pulled the lever. The bolt was withdrawn at three minutes past the hour and Langford dropped 7ft into the pit. Death was instant.

There is a sad footnote to the case. Langford's three children, aged 15, 13 and 10 were taken into the custody of a Dr Barnado's Home in Liverpool, but on the day before the execution, they were taken to separate homes in London to be away from the scene of their father's crime.

6

THE MAN WITH THE TWITCH

William Miller, 4 June 1895

On the evening of 18 February 1895, 15-year-old Johnny Needham answered the door at the house where he lived at 26 Redcross Street, Liverpool. Needham was an apprentice and worked in the house, which also doubled as an antiquarian bookshop. The caller asked to see the owner, Edward Moyse, an old man who, besides dealing in books from his home, also ran a bookstall at Mann Island on the banks of the Mersey. Moyse was a recluse and a rumour locally was that he was a very wealthy man.

The caller was welcomed into the house and shown into the kitchen. While waiting for the old man, he asked the boy if Moyse kept money in the house and if he used a bank. Needham said he did not know and before he could be questioned further, Moyse entered the room.

The man left after a short time, only to return within the hour. The two men were drinking in the kitchen when Needham retired to bed. At 5 a.m. on the following morning, Needham rose to prepare a fire and breakfast for his master but had been awake barely a few minutes when the stranger entered his room and asked him where the coal was stored as he wished to prepare a fire. Needham took him to the scullery whereupon the man picked up an axe and battered him about the head, knocking him to the ground. When the boy came to his senses, he staggered upstairs and found the brutally bludgeoned body of Edward Moyse on his bed. Having survived the murderous attack, Needham raised the alarm and was able to tell detectives that although he didn't know the name of the assailant, he did, however, have a pronounced twitch.

William Miller, the man with the twitch. (*T.J. Leech Archive*)

Following an intensive investigation that hit the headlines of newspapers in Liverpool and across the country, police eventually called at a house on Edgeware Street and arrested 27-year-old William Miller, an able seaman by profession. A search of his house unearthed a bloodstained shirt and although he claimed the bloodstains had been caused by his work in a slaughterhouse, this was soon found to be false.

Miller had a noticeable twitch and when he was put in a line-up of men and paraded before the bedside of the young Needham, the boy began to shake in fear and became hysterical as he indicated Miller as the murderer. It was purely on the testimony of Johnny Needham that William Miller found himself before Mr Justice Hawkins at Liverpool Assizes on Monday 13 May.

Miller denied the murder but the prosecution claimed that the prisoner had committed the crime for gain because he was penniless and being chased to repay money he had swindled from a woman. In the previous year Miller had met a wealthy widow in Edinburgh and they had eloped together to Philadelphia. While in America, Miller stole over £100 from her and headed back to Liverpool where his wife and children were now living.

Discovering the theft, the woman, now almost penniless, sold her clothes to buy her passage back to Liverpool where she tracked down Miller. She then went to the police who told her they were powerless to act as the alleged theft had taken place in another country.

In a letter Miller had written to his wife shortly before his arrest, he told her that he planned to poison himself with laudanum. Throughout his time in the death cell, Miller insisted he was not guilty of the murder, and at the last meeting with his wife, he insisted he was innocent and was in tears throughout the meeting. He went to his death with the same tears in his eyes and still protesting his innocence.

7

THE RAILWAY THIEVES

Elijah Winstanley, 17 December 1895

To combat the growing number of night-time thefts from railway wagons parked at Kay's House sidings, close to Chapel Lane, Wigan, the London North West Railway decided to try to catch the thieves in action by stationing extra railway policemen at the depot.

Early on the evening of Sunday 3 September 1895, it was the turn of Detective Sergeant Robert Kidd, a Salford-born father of seven, and his colleague Detective Constable William Osborne, and together they left their headquarters in Manchester and travelled by train to Wigan, arriving just after 7 p.m. Dressed in plain clothes and armed with only a truncheon and handcuffs, they secreted themselves out of sight and waited to see if anything happened.

After almost an hour of boredom, they decided to patrol the sidings and as they made their way slowly along the tracks, they heard sounds coming from one of the nearby wagons. Edging their way slowly towards the wagon, they spotted a man cutting through the ropes on a heavy tarpaulin to see what was concealed beneath.

Osbourne was first to the scene and spoke to the thief: 'Hello, what's going on here then?'

Without pausing from his endeavours the man simply replied: 'What is it to you?' And at that a number of other men sprung out from beneath the wagons and began to attack the officers. The melee was short and brutal. Massively outnumbered, the officers stood no chance and as Kidd tried to put his handcuffs on one of the men, he received several knife wounds to the chest and head. Osbourne was also knocked to the ground and as heavy clogs were aimed at his head and upper body, he curled into a ball and waited for the assault to end. Within seconds, the gang had fled towards the nearby Kay's Houses and as Osbourne clambered gingerly to his feet, he found his colleague on all fours bleeding profusely.

They managed to attract the attention of a railwayman in the nearby signal box and both were rushed to hospital where DS Kidd, who had been stabbed so many times it was impossible to count the wounds, soon died from his injuries.

Detectives centred their enquiries on nearby Kay's Houses. In recent months, a number of residents in these run-down slum cottages had come before the courts, and it seemed a natural place to begin enquiries. Within days they had a number of likely suspects who were taken to DS Osborne's bedside and paraded in front of the wounded officer. He was positively able to identify three men as having been involved in the fracas and murder: 31-year-old Elijah Winstanley; his 40-year-old stepbrother William Kearsley and William Halliwell, also aged 40. Placed under arrest, Winstanley immediately confessed that it was he alone that had committed the murder.

Nevertheless, all three men found themselves before Mr Justice Collins at Liverpool Assizes on Tuesday 26 November. Winstanley and Kearsley were charged with wilful murder; Halliwell, who had turned King's evidence against his two erstwhile friends, was charged with attempted robbery. Halliwell was the first to give evidence and collapsed in a faint when called to the dock. He was carried out of court and proceedings continued in his absence.

Despite Winstanley maintaining that it was his hand alone that had yielded the fatal blow, both were convicted of murder and sentenced to death. A week before sentence was carried out, Kearsley's conviction was commuted to life imprisonment, and Winstanley alone went to the gallows.

8

MITIGATING CIRCUMSTANCES?

Thomas Lloyd, 18 August 1897

Officers with the Liverpool City Police Force were frequent visitors to the house at 39 Tillard Street, Liverpool. Thomas Lloyd, a 55-year-old boilermaker, and his wife, Julia shared a house with several other families, one of whom, the McDowells, occupied rooms on the same floor. Lloyd and his wife did not have a happy marriage; both were addicted to hard drink and when drunk, they would fight with each other. These drunken brawls had resulted in officers being summoned to the house on many occasions, and usually the threat of arrest was enough for them to curb their tempers. Several times Lloyd and his wife had parted, sometimes for weeks on end as a result of their quarrels.

On 19 June 1897, Lloyd had been apart from his wife for several days and had decided to return home. To obtain courage to face the wrath of his wife, he stopped off at a local public house and, after consuming several pints, he sought the help of a friend whom he asked to pacify her and allow him to come back.

Lloyd was correct in assuming his wife would be angry. When he approached the front door she accused him of having been with another woman and laid into him with fists and feet as he tried to hold her at bay, fending off the blows until she relented and allowed him inside.

Across the landing, the McDowalls watched from the doorway and assumed things would soon go back to normal. True to form, strong language and drunken threats came from the Lloyds' room for most of the evening until Mrs McDowall heard Julia Lloyd tell her husband she was going to bed, swearing and calling him names as she slammed the door.

Footsteps were heard on the stairs and a short time later, Lloyd was seen holding an axe. On the following morning Mrs Lloyd was found seriously wounded from a number of head injuries caused by an axe. Of Thomas Lloyd there was now no sight.

The hunt for Lloyd lasted almost a week before he was spotted in the city centre and taken into custody. He denied attacking his wife but told detectives that if he had done it, he was prepared to 'swing for her like a man'. While Lloyd was held in custody, things got considerably worse for him when his wife Julia died of her injuries. Now charged with murder, he withdrew his confession and claimed, 'I never struck her, and nobody saw me strike her.'

At Liverpool Assizes before Mr Justice Bruce at the end of July, Lloyd pleaded mitigating circumstances and claimed that her bad temper had provoked him into committing the crime while in a drunken rage. His counsel asked for a verdict of manslaughter, but the jury were directed that the evidence as presented in court allowed for a verdict of guilty or not guilty of murder. The jury took twenty minutes to return a verdict of guilty of murder.

9

'NO OTHER MAN SHALL HAVE HER'

James Joseph Bergin, 27 December 1900

It was a conflict of religious beliefs that had caused the breakdown of the relationship between James Bergin and Margaret 'Maggie' Morrison. They had been courting for three years and had even fixed a date in December 1898 for their wedding when a series of events resulted in the postponement of the wedding plans and an eventual murder charge.

The first problem arose when Bergin lost his job in the autumn of 1898. The loss of income meant a reassessment of their immediate future and as a result, the impending wedding was postponed and rescheduled for the following year. Arrangements for a new date then caused arguments in their families. Bergin's family were staunch Roman Catholics, while Maggie and her relations were all members of the Protestant Church.

Although the first date for the wedding had been set without much being said, this time the quarrels between the families became so heated that the nuptials, set for a few days before Christmas 1899, were postponed indefinitely. Soon after, Bergin left Liverpool and returned to his family in Ireland.

Three months later, in July 1900, he returned to Liverpool and immediately sought out Maggie Morrison. Mindful of the harsh words and unpleasant scenes the last time the couple met, her mother refused him entry to the house, adding that Maggie wished to have nothing more to do with him. Bergin brooded over what she had said and as he turned to leave, he made a chilling remark: 'I'll take her life and no other man shall have her!' When Mrs Morrison threatened to call the police, Bergin was defiant, claiming that he was prepared to do twenty years for her if need be.

Two days later, he made another visit to Maggie's home in Bootle. This time her family seemed to accept their daughter's wish to speak with Bergin and he was welcomed in and offered tea. Mrs Morrison allowed them to talk alone in the parlour while she and another daughter retired to the kitchen.

Suddenly there were sounds of a disturbance and, rushing into the parlour, Mrs Morrison found Bergin, his trousers burnt and smoking from carbolic acid, confronted by an angry Maggie, wielding a razor. The bizarre tableau was interrupted and Bergin was ordered out of the house.

On 20 October, a drunken Bergin returned to the Morrison house but was told by Maggie's mother that she was not at home. Bergin was not convinced and declared loudly that he had heard her voice before he had knocked on the door. 'Remember Mrs Morrison' he said coldly, 'she is your daughter and if any other man walks out with her, I shall take her life.'

One week later, on 27 October, Maggie and her mother were in Stanley Road, Bootle, when they met Bergin. He accompanied them to Liverpool where they all met up with Maggie's father. As they reached the city centre, Bergin said he wished to take Maggie to the Haymarket Theatre and, somewhat surprisingly in view of recent events, the Morrisons gave their consent.

At 11 p.m. Maggie and Bergin were strolling arm in arm down Bankhall Street, heading for the Morrison house. A few paces behind walked a man and his son, also making their way home. Suddenly, they heard a loud bang followed by a flash of bright light. Maggie fell to the pavement and Bergin crouched down beside her, whereupon there was another loud bang and a flash.

The man and his son shouted and gave chase. They were able to identify the assailant, but lost him in the maze of narrow streets. On Bankhall Street, Maggie Morrison lay still on the pavement; she had been shot twice in the head and fatally wounded. She died from her injuries in hospital two days later, by which time Bergin was in custody, charged with attempted murder.

At Bergin's trial before Mr Justice Darling, his counsel Mr (later Mr Justice) Rigby Swift claimed that the prisoner was insane and offered evidence that three members of Bergin's family had previously been certified insane. This was refuted and the prosecution pointed to the threat Bergin had made to Mrs Morrison on his return from Ireland. The court was told how Bergin had sworn to kill Maggie if she failed to resume their relationship and he had boasted that he was prepared to serve twenty years for it. This proved that the prisoner was aware of the consequences of his actions and destroyed his defence that he was insane at the time of the killing and unaware of his actions. The jury duly returned the expected guilty verdict but added a recommendation to mercy.

Above left: James Joseph Bergin. (*T.J. Leech Archive*)

Above right: Margaret Morrison, shot dead by James Bergin. (*T.J. Leech Archive*)

10

HORROR AT ROSE COTTAGE

John Harrison, 24 December 1901

Rose Cottage was a deserted bungalow standing on farmland at the top end of Bickerstaffe Moss. At 9.45 a.m. on Saturday 27 July 1901, farmer Peter Marsh was approached by a woman and asked if he owned the cottage down the lane, and if so, was it available for rent? Told that it was, she said her name was Alice Wright and asked if she could rent it. Marsh accompanied her back to the cottage where he saw a man, who gave his name as John Harrison. They agreed terms and the pair were given the keys to the unfurnished cottage.

At ten past one that afternoon, Harrison was seen walking away from the cottage, avoiding making eye contact with a passer by, and hanging his head down as if to avoid being recognised. Ten minutes later, Rachael Coxhead, who lived nearby, passed the cottage and, noticing a window was smashed, went to investigate. Peering inside, she saw a woman lying on the floor, but assuming it was just a drunk looking for somewhere to sleep off a hangover, she went on her way.

At 9 p.m. that night, Harrison called at Rose Farm and in a highly distressed state, told Marsh he had found his wife dead at the cottage. Marsh advised him to inform the police at Skelmersdale, which Harrison accordingly did, and officers arrived at the cottage a few minutes before midnight.

Alice Wright was found lying at the foot of two steps between the ground-floor rooms in the cottage. There were marks of violence around her neck and she was lying in a pool of blood, which came from a deep cut on her hand. The cause of death was due to strangulation. Harrison had bloodstains on his shirtsleeve and under his thumbnail and, suspecting he may be responsible for her death, officers placed him under arrest while investigations were carried out into the dead woman's recent movements.

Alice Wright was a married woman, separated from her husband, who had bigamously married Harrison, a 31-year-old collier, a few months earlier. They led what police termed 'a very irregular life', wandering around the villages of West Lancashire, where Harrison did casual work while Alice earned a little money from prostitution to pay for their lodgings. The previous evening prior to turning up at Rose Cottage, they had been together in Ormskirk and, failing to find a room for the night, they had then walked on to Skelmersdale. They were seen early on the following morning, drinking in the Engine Inn, before setting off in the direction of Bickerstaffe. Witnesses at the public house told officers that the couple had had some sort of argument there.

Harrison claimed that he had left the cottage at around 2 p.m. and walked to St Helens where he had been drinking at the Prince of Wales Inn with a bookmaker named Harry Dingwall. Dingwall told the officer that he had indeed been in the pub, but denied having met Harrison there at any time that day.

This was enough for detectives to charge Harrison with wilful murder and on 2 December, he appeared before Mr Justice Bucknill at Liverpool Assizes. Although the evidence against him was circumstantial, it nevertheless needed explaining. Harrison's claim that he had left the house at 2 p.m. contradicted the testimony of Rachael Coxhead who said that forty minutes earlier, she had looked into the cottage and saw a woman lying on the floor, and the witness who claimed to have seen Harrison walking away from the cottage ten minutes before Mrs Coxhead peered through the window.

Although the court heard of the alleged argument between the couple on the morning of the murder, there was no other evidence or known motive for Harrison to strangle Alice Wright, but the jury needed just an hour to find him guilty as charged.

John Harrison was hanged at Walton Prison on Christmas Eve, allegedly protesting his innocence to the end.

11

THE ESTRANGED HUSBAND

Thomas Marsland, 20 May 1902

It took less than three months for Elizabeth Marsland to realise her marriage to Thomas Marsland was a mistake. They had tied the knot at Oldham Registry Office on 23 November 1901, and took lodgings at 40 Edge Lane Hollow, Royton. From the start, Marsland ill-treated his wife, slapping and punching her whenever they had any sort of disagreement, and his behaviour was too much for their landlady, Hannah Lowe, who, having witnessed one particular assault, ordered the couple out of her home.

Hannah Lowe warned Elizabeth to be careful and not to stand for his brutal treatment. She took heed of the advice and by February 1902, the Marslands had parted and Elizabeth moved to 1 Horsedge Fold, Oldham. She found a job as a cleaner at the offices belonging to her new next-door neighbour, James Kelly, on Union Street.

Elizabeth kept in touch with Hannah Lowe and that Easter she returned to Royton and stayed with her former landlady for several days. On the morning of Friday 4 April, she went to work and was seen by her employer talking to her estranged husband outside the Greaves Arms on Yorkshire Street.

That afternoon Marsland bought himself a new razor. At 6.15 p.m. Elizabeth Marsland returned home, stopping to chat to her neighbour, Mrs Kelly, before entering her own house. At 7.30 p.m. Mrs Kelly heard a number of screams coming from next door but for some reason, did not go to investigate. They stopped moments later and there was no sound from the house until half an hour later when the front door slammed and Mrs Kelly saw Elizabeth's husband lock the door, light up a cigarette and set off down the street.

At 8.20 p.m., Police Constable Michael Conway was on his beat near the Mumps railway station when Marsland approached him looking agitated. 'I have to come to give myself up for murdering my wife' he told the startled officer.

Back at the station, Marsland, who gave his occupation as a piecer in a local cotton mill, told detectives that his wife had left him and, unaware she had gone to visit Hannah Lowe in Royton, he had grown increasing angry at not being able to find her. He said that after seeing her earlier that morning, he had gone to her house and waited for her to return home. When she returned, they had had a quarrel and he struck her with a rolling pin before cutting her throat with the newly purchased razor.

Marsland's trial before Mr Justice Walton at Liverpool Assizes was held less than a month after the murder. Marsland was clearly resigned to his fate. Not only did he make a full

Estranged husband Thomas Marsland.
(*T.J. Leech Archive*)

confession to the crime, but when the shopkeeper who sold him the razor failed to recognise him in an identity parade, Marsland came to his assistance. 'That's the man who sold me the razor!' he shouted out as the startled shopkeeper reached the end of the parade, 'I paid one shilling for it!'

12

THE *VERONICA* MUTINEERS

Gustav Rau & Willem Schmidt, 2 June 1903

The *Veronica* was a three-masted British-registered ship, which, in the autumn of 1902, was bound for Montevideo. On 11 October, with a mixed nations' crew of twelve, she left Ship Island in the Gulf of Mexico with a cargo of timber. What happened during the journey has never been clearly explained.

On Christmas Day 1902, under the command of Captain George Browne, the SS *Brunswick* dropped anchor at Cajueira Island in the mouth of Paranhyba River, Brazil. The ship was to be in port for three days before commencing a return voyage to Liverpool, via a number of Portuguese ports. On the final day in port, as the last of the cargo was being secured in the holds, a small lifeboat with the name *Veronica* clearly inscribed, pulled up alongside.

There were five men in the boat: 28-year-old Gustav Rau, a former sailor in the German Navy; Otto Monsson and Henry Flohr, also German; 30-year-old Dutchman Willem Schmidt; and Moses Thomas, a young American Negro.

Rau told Captain Browne that their last voyage had been traumatic: two men had died as a result of accidents and a few days ago, fire had broken out in Captain Shaw's quarters, forcing them to abandon ship. Two lifeboats had been launched but they had soon lost sight of the other boat.

Their story was initially accepted and the men were taken aboard and promised a safe passage back to Liverpool. No sooner had they set sail than Moses Thomas asked to speak to Captain Browne and told a remarkable story.

Claiming that his life was in danger, he said that Rau's story was false and that the other four men were mutineers who had murdered the captain and the remainder of the crew on the *Veronica*. He said that Rau had already tried to strangle him when they had been allocated their quarters and Thomas asked to be housed somewhere else on the ship until they reached port.

Thomas said that one of the crew on the *Veronica*, an Irishman named Paddy Doran, had quarrelled with Rau and a fight had broken out. Rau came off worst. Later that day, Rau and Willem Schmidt had battered Doran to death with lumps of metal, before hiding his body in the paint store. The disturbance alerted the attention of other members of the crew and the two men also attacked them. Thomas said that the mutineers had shot dead the captain and battered or shot dead six other crewmen. Thomas said they had only spared his life because he was the ship's cook and had played no part in any of the fighting on deck.

The Veronica Mutiny and Murders

DOUBLE EXECUTION IN LIVERPOOL.

PROTESTATION ON THE SCAFFOLD.

Newspaper cutting reporting the execution of the *Veronica* Mutineers. (*Author's collection*)

Above left: Gustav Rau. (*Author's collection*)

Above right: Willem Schmidt. (*Author's collection*)

Moses Thomas with a replica of the *Veronica* at Liverpool Assizes. (*Liverpool County Record Office*)

When the ship reached Lisbon, the captain sought advice from the British consulate and they decided to wait until they reached Liverpool before informing the rescued sailors of the allegations.

On arrival at Liverpool's Herculaneum Dock, police officers boarded the ship and took Rau and his three companions into custody. Under questioning, all four changed their story, now naming Moses Thomas as the leader of the mutiny and the man solely responsible for carrying out the mass murder. Detectives did not believe this account and when Henry Flohr turned King's evidence, the other three men, Rau, Schmidt and Monsson, were charged with seven counts of murder, piracy and conspiracy.

Tried for just the murder of Captain Shaw, the three men appeared before Mr Justice Lawrance at Liverpool Assizes in May. The trial lasted three days and ended with all three defendants being found guilty and sentenced to death. In the case of 18-year-old Otto Monsson, the jury added a recommendation to mercy, on account of his youth. This was quickly accepted by the Secretary of State who sanctioned a reprieve.

Rau and Schmidt were hanged side by side in the first double execution to take place at Walton. They had been kept apart since conviction and met up for the first time as they were led to the gallows. They didn't speak to each other, although Rau spoke his last words to the hangman: 'I am innocent of the murders of those men,' he told William Billington as the noose was placed around his neck.

13

THE MAINTENANCE ORDER

Henry Bertram Starr, 29 December 1903

Mr Justice Ridley completed his summing up and invited the jury to consider their verdict. It was the evening of Monday 7 December 1903, and there was murmuring in the gallery as the jury stayed seated and began to talk in whispers. The prisoner was still in the dock waiting to be escorted below when moments later, the foreman made it known to the clerk that they had agreed on their verdict. In an unusual end to the trial, the clerk draped a black cap on the judge's wig and sentence of death was passed on the shocked prisoner.

Thirty-one-year-old Henry Starr had married his wife, Mary in the spring of 1903. Expecting their first child, the couple spent the first few months of marriage living with her mother at Blackpool before something occurred that was to have a profound effect on the relationship. Starr began to drink heavily and eventually things became so strained that he moved out.

In early August, Mary gave birth to their child and within days, Starr asked her to come and live with him and to try to salvage their relationship. Mary agreed but by November, she had returned to her mother, half-starved and complaining of being mistreated by her husband.

On 16 November Mary received a letter from Starr, asking her to return to him. Starr seemingly suspected she wouldn't agree to this request so concluded the letter with a threat that if she refused, he intended to apply for custody of their child. Mary countered this by consulting a solicitor and on his advice, obtained a separation order, a custody order for the child and for good measure, took out a maintenance order for 6s a week against her estranged husband.

Starr was enraged and decided on drastic action. On the following day, Tuesday 24 November, he called at her mother's house. Mary went downstairs to answer the door and a few moments later, her mother heard Mary cry out: 'Help! Murder!' When her mother hurried downstairs into the front room, she found Mary lying on the hearthrug with Starr standing over her, holding a bloodstained knife, which he continued to thrust into the stricken, prone body of his wife. Mary's mother rushed at Starr, knocking the knife from his hand. Starr fled into the kitchen, snatched up another knife and returned to the front room and struck out at his mother-in-law, seriously wounding her. Instead of finishing her off, Starr suddenly put down his knife and let the unfortunate woman stagger out into the street and call for help.

By the time the police arrived, Starr had fled but was soon tracked down to a nearby public house. With blood on his hands and clothing, he denied the murder and claimed he had been involved in a bar-room brawl.

At his trial, evidence was heard that witnesses had seen Starr wandering the streets close to his home on the night before the attack, murmuring to himself and making threats to 'do it!' His defence claimed that he had been suffering from delirium tremens (DTs), and a friend testified that Starr had definitely been suffering from this on Saturday night.

The prosecution claimed simply that Starr had been driven to commit the murder having been angered at the maintenance order taken out against him, and that while he may have been suffering from DTs on Saturday night, it was asking a lot to believe he was still suffering three days later when he committed the brutal murder and the attempted murder. The jury clearly believed this was the case and needed less than a minute to reach their verdict.

It was the second time that Starr had been on trial for his life. Seven years earlier he had been acquitted of the murder of a woman in Clitheroe. This time he went to the gallows.

Above left: Henry Bertram Starr. (*T.J. Leech Archive*)

Above right: Mary Starr, stabbed to death by her husband. (*T.J. Leech Archive*)

14

THE SISTER-IN-LAW

William Kirwan, 31 May 1904

Since his arrest for murder, sailor William Kirwan hadn't held out much hope of a successful outcome to his trial. After all, he had committed a brutal murder in front of several witnesses, not least a police constable who had been called to deal with a fracas. As Mr Justice Bucknill completed his summing up at Liverpool Assizes on Monday 9 May 1904, the jury were invited to go and consider their verdict in a room put aside for them. Without leaving their seats, they merely looked across at each other and nodded to the foreman, who then leaned over and told the clerk they had reached their verdict. Kirwan stood impassively as they found him guilty as charged and with the black cap draped on his wig, the judge sentenced him to be hanged by the neck until dead.

Thirty-nine-year-old Kirwan was a merchant seaman on the transatlantic routes and as a result, he often spent long periods away at sea. On shore leave in February 1904, he was told that his wife, Sarah and her 25-year-old sister, Mary Pike, had been working as prostitutes and had been using Mary's home on Great Newton Street for immoral purposes.

On the afternoon of Friday 26 February 1904, Kirwan obtained a revolver and followed his wife to her sister's house. He stood in a doorway across the street and waited to see if the stories about her were true. A short time later a man came out of the front door and walked off down the street. Now convinced that the house was being used for prostitution, Kirwan stormed up to the front door, burst inside and confronted them. Both denied the accusations but Kirwan was not convinced.

A fierce quarrel ensued and as they came to blows, Kirwan pulled out his gun and fired four shots. The first two, aimed at his sister-in-law, missed their target, the third bullet grazed the arm of his wife, and the last shot, accidentally discharged during the struggle, missed its target and struck the wall. A lodger at the house intervened, bundled Mrs Pike's children into the cellar and pushed Mrs Kirwan into the lobby.

Kirwan then walked out into the street and ordered his wife home. He continued making threats until a policeman arrived and sizing up the situation, he restrained Kirwan and took hold of his arm. Feeling that the threat of danger had subsided, Mary Pike emerged from the house and began to berate Kirwan. It was a fatal mistake. The officer was unaware that Kirwan had a gun in his pocket and was helpless as Kirwan suddenly freed himself from the grip, took a few paces into the road and pulled out the gun. He pointed it at Mary Pike and pulled the trigger, mortally wounding his sister-in-law.

His defence at the trial pleaded guilty of manslaughter under extreme provocation, but a brief statement that Kirwan had made to the officer called to deal with the disturbance, that he intended to kill both his wife and her sister, proved decisive.

15

THE GAMBLING DEN MURDER

Pong Lun, 31 May 1904

The large, rambling tenement building on Frederick Street in Liverpool's Chinese Quarter was a lodging house mainly for Chinese sailors and dockworkers. The cellar of the house was also a popular meeting place for other Chinamen who would visit the house to chat with friends, smoke and drink, but mainly to gamble. Amongst those who took lodgings there was Pong Lun, a 43-year-old storekeeper at the docks, who had been a tenant there since the summer of 1903, and who, like many of his friends, was an avid gambler.

On the evening of Sunday 24 March 1904, the cellar at Frederick Street was packed. The air was thick with opium and tobacco smoke and a crowd was gathered around four men who were playing and gambling on a game played with dominoes. One of the players, 29-year-old John Go Hing, a close friend of Lun's, was acting as a banker and it was at Hing's discretion when bets could be laid during the game.

A game was already under way when Lun entered the cellar and edged towards the gaming table. He watched several games before deciding to place a bet on the hand of another of his friends, Moy Chung. Lun leaned over the table and placed a number of chips, only for Go Hing to brush them aside saying it was too late to place any more bets. Lun insisted he was able to place the bet, but Go Hing was adamant that he was too late. Lun then watched in a rage as the game ended and as his bet would have come up and yielded him a tidy sum.

He demanded to be paid, but Go Hing was firm and waved away his plea, saying the bet had been too late. Lun stormed out of the room, only to return several minutes later, again demanding that his winning bet be settled. Go Hing had now relinquished the banker's chair to another gambler and was standing next to a fireplace lighting his pipe when Lun pulled out a gun and fired two shots. The first whistled past his shoulder, the second struck Go Hing in the stomach, fatally wounding him.

Lun then wielded the gun threatening to shoot anyone who got in his way as he fled the scene. He was arrested later that night when he returned to his lodgings, and was charged with attempted murder, although when Go Hing succumbed to his injuries three days later, the charge was changed to one of murder.

Lun stood trial before Mr Justice Bucknill on 10 May at Liverpool Assizes. Unusually for an English court of law, all the evidence was given in Chinese and translated into English by interpreters. The oath was also different from the usual form of swearing on the Bible; instead, witnesses smashed a saucer and declared: 'As this saucer is broken, if I do not speak the truth so may my soul be broken hereafter.'

The trial was a formality. The prosecution called a number of witnesses who had all been present when the shooting took place. Lun was hanged by William Billington and Henry Pierrepoint in a double execution, alongside William Kirwan (*see* chapter 14).

Pierrepoint later recalled an amusing tale on the night concerning the execution. He said that as the hangmen slept in their quarters in what was the old hospital, a few steps from the scaffold, he had awoken to find a swarm of mice on both their beds. 'Wake up Billy, you're

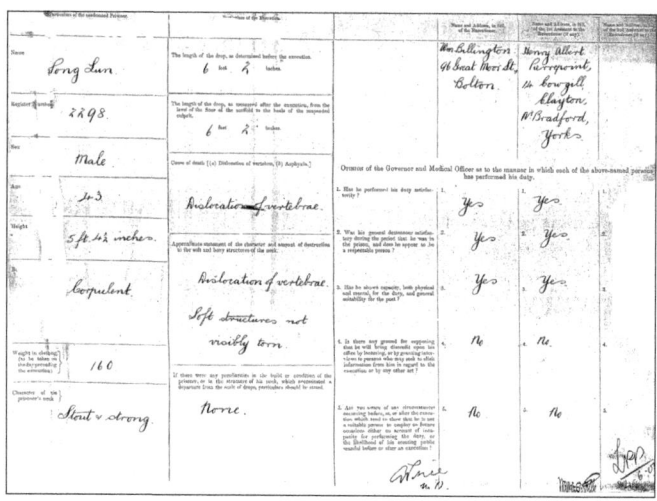

Above left: William Billington, who took over from his father as chief executioner. (*Author's collection*)

Above right: Pong Lun's record of execution. (*Author's collection*)

being worried by mice!' he shouted to his friend and they spent the next hour laughing and clearing the room of mice.

On the following morning, as Billington entered the condemned cell and pinioned the Chinaman, he commented cheerily: 'Come on Ping Pong!' At this the prisoner turned to him and bristled, replying: 'My name not Ping Pong. It is Pong Lun.'

Lun was alleged to have burst out laughing as they entered the gallows' chamber when he saw Kirwan already noosed and ready, and the other rope waiting for him.

16

THE LODGER

Charles Patterson, 7 August 1907

George Charlton was polishing his boots and trying to ignore the quarrel that was taking place between his mother and 37-year-old, half-caste sailor, Charles Patterson in the kitchen of the small terrace house on Crondall Street, in Manchester's Moss Side. It was the evening of Saturday 29 June 1907, and the quarrel, which had begun at lunchtime, was about lodger Patterson's failure to pay the rent he had promised, and which was now well overdue.

It seems the relationship between Patterson and his landlady, 39-year-old Mrs Lillian Jane Charlton, was more than just landlord and tenant. Patterson had often shared her bed and in his eyes, this meant he was no longer a paying guest and should not be liable to pay for his room. In previous months when he had been out of work, Mrs Charlton appeared to have allowed the rent to go unpaid, but now that he had found work on the Manchester Ship Canal, he was back in his own room, and she needed the money to pay for his share of the food, heating and other costs.

There was also another reason. The relationship between landlady and lodger had deteriorated in recent weeks, due mainly to Patterson's aggressive and brutal manner. He would often strike out at her when he lost his temper and she had made enquiries about having a warrant taken out against him for assault. A warrant cost money, which she did not have, but with the rent due she would be able to take steps to get him evicted.

As the quarrel escalated, Mrs Charlton finally lost her patience. She told him to pack his bags and find somewhere else to live. Not only that, but she said that if he didn't pay the rent due she would take out proceedings against him. She then slammed the kitchen door and stormed upstairs. A few minutes later Patterson came out of the kitchen and followed Lillian upstairs. Moments later a scream rang out. George darted up the stairs and found the bathroom door locked. He shouted for Patterson to open the door and when he refused, he kicked it open. He was horrified to find Patterson, standing by the bath, with a grotesque smile on his face and clutching a bloodstained razor. George's mother was lying in a pool of blood on the bathroom floor with a large gash on her throat.

How the *Illustrated Police News* reported the murder of Lillian Charlton. (*T.J. Leech Archive*)

Above left: Charles Patterson. (*T.J. Leech Archive*)

Above right: Hangman Henry Pierrepoint carried out two executions at Walton. (*Author's collection*)

George ran for help and a neighbour hurried back and found that Mrs Charlton had died from her injuries. Patterson had, in the meantime, left the house and stood calmly in the back yard waiting for the police to arrive. He asked one of the neighbours for a piece of chewing tobacco before he was taken away under arrest.

Patterson confessed to the murder when taken to the police station and when he appeared before Mr Justice Channell at Liverpool Assizes on 15 July, this confession formed the basis of the prosecution case. In the event, there was no case to prove. Patterson chose to plead guilty to the charge of murder and, as he did from the moment of his arrest, he seemed indifferent to his fate. This led to the defence counsel putting forward a plea that Patterson was insane, but Dr Price, the prison doctor at Walton, took the stand and testified that he had spoke at length with the prisoner and there was nothing to suggest any sign of insanity.

17

RIVALS

See Lee, 30 March 1909

The railway policeman noticed a man acting suspiciously on Platform 1 at Liverpool's Lime Street station and, after watching his movements for several minutes, went to investigate.

It was just after 10 p.m. on Saturday 5 December 1908, and William Miller was doing the rounds of the station, moving along drunks and vagrants, when he noticed a Chinese man behaving in a strange manner. Miller approached and spoke to him, asking him what he was doing and was told by the man that he was waiting for the train to Glasgow, before travelling to Hong Kong.

The man appeared to be drunk and as Miller continued patrolling, he decided to keep him under observation. The next train for Glasgow was not due for almost three hours and at 12.30 a.m., just fifteen minutes before the scheduled departure time, Miller saw the man enter the booking hall. He again went to speak to him and this time noticed that he was carrying a sailor's pay book bearing the name See Lee. Lee's name had been mentioned earlier that evening as being wanted in connection with an attempted murder that had taken place on the previous day and, as a result, the man was detained and taken in for questioning.

In the winter of December 1908, widow Amy Yap Sing had been bedridden for almost two months with peritonitis. Following the death of her Chinese-born husband in the summer of 1908, London-born Amy had run their lodging house at 13 Dickinson Street, Liverpool, alone. She was not, however, without visitors, and in particular, two Chinese sailors seemed to be vying for her attention.

Forty-year-old Yun Yap, and See Lee, aged 38, had become friends when they shared lodgings in Cardiff in 1904. It was in the Welsh port that Yap had also met Amy Yap Sing, when she moved from London to run a boarding house, and they had met up again when he found work for a Liverpool shipping company. Amy had by now moved to Liverpool and Yap later took up a job as a cook at Amy and her husband's lodging house at 36 Pitt Street, close to the Liverpool docks.

See Lee had met Amy when he came to Liverpool in January 1908 and by that winter, Amy had been taken ill and both Yun Yap and See Lee had made frequent visits to her bedside. On Thursday 3 December, both men visited Amy at the same time. Leaving the bedroom, they went down to the kitchen, where they shared a few drinks and eventually parted on seemingly good terms.

On the following evening, Lee returned to visit Amy and stayed for a quarter of an hour. Later that night, shortly after 9 p.m., Yap called to see Amy. He was standing at the foot of her bed when Lee returned. Without speaking a word, Lee stared at the scene before him, and then pulled out a pistol and shot Yap in the chest. As his compatriot collapsed, mortally wounded on the bed, Lee turned and walked out of the house.

Rushed to the nearby hospital, Yap made a statement naming his assailant and claiming he had no idea why he had been shot. Lee had already been detained in custody when Yap died from his wounds three days later.

Tried before Lord Chief Justice Alverstone at Liverpool Assizes on 12 March 1909, Lee denied murder and claimed that the shooting was accidental and had happened during a fight. He claimed that Yap had been jealous of his friendship with Amy and when he had entered her bedroom, Yap had pulled out a gun and warned him off. He tried to wrestle the gun from his hand and it had gone off accidentally. Lee's version of events did not agree with the testimony of Amy Yap Sing and the jury, believing that Lee, driven by jealousy, had shot his former friend and rival, returned the only verdict open to them.

It was not See Lee's first time in the dock at Liverpool Assizes. Five years before, he had been present in a gambling den when his friend Pong Lun had shot dead John Go Hing. Lee had been one of the prosecution witnesses called and his statement had helped send Lun to the same gallows Lee was to also end his life on.

18

AT THE SECOND ATTEMPT

Henry Thompson, 22 November 1910

'Never was such callousness exhibited by a man sentenced to death' ran a Sunday newspaper report into the trial of 54-year-old former marine fireman Henry Thompson, who had been charged with the murder of his wife in the autumn of 1910. Having been found guilty by the jury, the clerk of the Assizes asked the prisoner if he had anything to say as to why sentence of death should not be passed Thompson replied: 'No, let 'em go ahead with it. I don't care. I never was frightened of death.'

With the black cap draped on his wig Mr Justice Avory prepared to address the prisoner. 'Henry Thompson,' he began with deep solemnity. 'Yes, my Lord? I'm not guilty!' the prisoner shouted. 'Silence!' cried one of the ushers.

Thompson turned to the bench and retorted: 'I'll not silence. I'm not guilty.' Then, after a moment's pause, he leaned over the rail of the dock and glared at the judge: 'You can sentence away now!'

When the solemn sentence concluded, Thompson thrust his hands into his pockets and shouted 'Amen!' As the warders closed in, he turned to his friends in the gallery, bade them farewell, and disappeared below the dock and out of sight.

Henry and Mary Thompson had married in 1902. It wasn't the happiest of unions as both were addicted to strong drink, and while Mary was quite placid, her husband was quarrelsome and violent. During a disagreement in 1904, Thompson lost his temper and tried to murder his wife, cutting her throat with a razor. Mary was able to receive medical attention and her life was saved. Thompson was arrested and charged with attempted murder, but with his wife's intervention, the charge was downgraded to assault and he served just a short term of imprisonment. On his release, Thompson returned home, seemingly to his wife's forgiveness, and they continued with their lives much as before.

In the summer of 1910, they took rooms at 18 York Road, Liverpool, sharing the house with another family, a married couple named Martin and Catherine Reynolds. On the night of Saturday 30 July, Thompson and his wife went out drinking and during the night, they separated and drank with their own friends.

When Mary came home later that night, Thompson was already there and he launched into a fierce verbal assault on her. 'You can go back to where you have been all night. If you come back into this house I will kill you stone dead. I have nearly hung once, and I will be hung for you before long.' It would prove to be a prophetic boast.

Thompson slammed the door on his wife, but a short time later he heard her enter the house and go to the Reynolds' room, asking if she could stay the night. They allowed her in but a short time later Thompson demanded to he see his wife. When told she wasn't there, he kicked at the door and made threats against Reynolds and his wife, and eventually Mary appeared at the door and Thompson grabbed her by the arm and propelled her towards their own room. Later they heard her cry, 'Oh Harry, don't choke me!'

On the following afternoon, Thompson asked Mrs Reynolds if she would go to the shop to purchase some whiskey to celebrate Mary's 47th birthday, which was that day. Having purchased the whiskey, Mrs Reynolds later prepared some sandwiches and offered to take them to Mary, who had not stirred. Thompson was unwilling to let her into the room and took them in himself.

A friend of Mary's was also refused entry to the bedroom when she called to see her, and on the Monday morning, concerned that something was amiss, Reynolds managed to gain entry to the Thompsons' bedroom. Henry Thompson was snoring in a deep sleep lying beside his wife, who was still dressed in the clothes she had been wearing on the previous night. It only took a touch of Mary's stone cold, bare flesh to realise she was dead and they hurried to fetch the police.

When officers arrived Thompson was still asleep and had to be roused awake to explain why his wife was dead. 'I don't know anything about this. The bloody thing was lying like a stuffed dummy in the bed beside me,' was all he would say. Medical examination would later show that she had been strangled.

At his trial, Thompson insisted that Mary must have died from some sort of fit in the night and that he had done nothing since finding her dead, fearing he would be blamed for her murder.

Following conviction, he remained callous and indifferent to his fate although he did show signs of contrition as the final days approached, telling guards that he was a Buddhist and would come back as a bird to see them all.

Thompson, who had tried once to murder his wife, and had succeeded at the second attempt, walked to the scaffold with an air of utter unconcern, and hangman Ellis later recorded that he never hanged a cooler man.

Callous murderer Henry Thompson, sketched in court shortly before he was sentenced to death. (*T.J. Leech Archive*)

19

THE OLD SAILOR

Thomas Seymour, 9 May 1911

Sixty-four-year-old Thomas Seymour had spent most of his life at sea, and it was while at home on leave at Liverpool in 1907 that he married his cousin, Mary. Seymour, whose real name had been McKillican, was a likeable man and popular with friends and neighbours, but that same amiability didn't, it seems, stretch to his marriage, which was fraught with bickering and quarrels. There were even relatives who wondered why they were together at all, speculating that it may have had more than a little to do with a large inheritance Mary had received shortly before they wed.

They moved into a house at 3 Breckfield Place, Everton, and although Mary Seymour was careful with money, once her husband had retired from the Merchant Navy and was now home every day, they soon frittered it away, mostly on drink. By Christmas 1910 there was hardly anything left, and with the money gone, so it seems had the last of Seymour's affections for his wife. He took to beating her often, usually when drunk, and her relatives were frequently telling her to pack her bags and leave him. Unfortunately, Mary chose to ignore them.

On the morning of Saturday 11 March 1911, Mary's sister, Elizabeth Jones, called at their house. After much knocking, Seymour eventually opened the door, but tried to refuse her entry, keeping her talking on the doorstep and trying to stall her. Elizabeth sensed something was

Old soldier Thomas Seymour.
(*T.J. Leech Archive*)

wrong and barged through the door into the front room where she was greeted with a horrific sight. Mary Seymour lay dead in the corner of the room having been battered to death by the bloodstained hammer that lay beside her body. Hot ashes had then been scattered over Mary's head, either to hasten death or soak up the blood. As Elizabeth Jones began to scream and shout at him, Seymour merely picked up his coat and said he was going to find a policeman.

Following his arrest, Seymour seemed oblivious to the consequences of his actions and admitted his guilt every time the crime was discussed. At his first hearing at the local magistrate's court, he even asked if the matter could be dealt with there and then instead of wasting his and the judge's time by sending it to the Assizes. The magistrate told Seymour that he had no power to deal with the matter, which had to be heard before a high court judge.

In due course Seymour appeared before Mr Justice Avory at Liverpool Assizes. The judge had been pre-warned that the prisoner was choosing to plead guilty to the charge and when Seymour stepped into the dock, the judge asked if he was aware of what he was pleading guilty to and the consequences of such a plea. Seymour said he did, and the judge then ordered him out of the dock while the matter was discussed with lawyers and to see if they could get the prisoner to try to defend himself. Seymour grew weary at the delay in getting the trial over and done with and when brought back into court and asked again by the judge if he still chose to plead guilty, and that he understood the implications of this, he snapped angrily, 'Of course I do!'

With proceedings quickly wrapped up, Seymour was taken to Walton where he remained truculent and untroubled by the severity of his situation. Twenty days after the conviction, the old sailor, who seemingly could not wait to die, had to wait no longer.

20

THE CHILD-KILLER

Michael Fagan, 6 December 1911

Twenty-seven-year-old dockworker Michael Fagan, his wife, Annie, and 4-year-old daughter lodged in the tiny terrace house at 128 Arlington Road, Liverpool, along with a widow named Mrs Crumby and a single mother, Mary Kennedy and her 2-year-old daughter, Lucy.

One Saturday, 9 September 1911, Annie Fagan and Mary Kennedy went out shopping together, leaving Lucy with Michael who promised to look after her while they were away. The two women became separated and Annie Fagan arrived back at Arlington Street first, at around 6 p.m. Her own daughter, also called Annie, tearfully greeted her with the dreadful news that: 'Daddy has been beating the baby.'

When Mary Kennedy herself arrived home an hour later, she was horrified to hear from the shaken and tearful Annie that something terrible had happened and when she entered the house she found Lucy lying unconscious on her mother's bed. She had clearly been badly assaulted: both eyes were blackened, she had cuts on her face, but more horrifying were the dreadful weals, cuts and bruising on the child's buttocks. A doctor was called and Lucy was rushed to Stanley Hospital where she died a few hours later.

Brutal child-killer Michael
Fagan. (*T.J. Leech Archive*)

Fagan had already fled the house before his wife arrived back home, but later that night, he
returned. Clearly drunk, he said that the child had cried incessantly and he had lost his temper, but
had merely slapped it with his belt. Shortly after midnight, police officers investigating what had now
become a murder enquiry, arrived at the house and found Fagan upstairs, lying on his bed, sobbing.
He was taken to the police station, where he admitted that he had struck Lucy with his belt.

When Fagan appeared before Mr Justice Avory at Liverpool Assizes on Wednesday
8 November, his defence was based around him being so drunk at the time of the attack, he had
no knowledge of his actions. The prosecution alleged that it was something far more sinister.
It was suggested that the prisoner had brutally violated the young child and had then attempted
to disguise the penetrative injuries by kicking and lashing out with his belt.

The jury needed just thirty minutes to return a guilty verdict to the charge of murder but
shocked the judge by adding a strong recommendation for mercy. 'On what grounds do you
make your recommendation for mercy?' the bewildered Avory asked the jury. Told that it was
on the grounds of the alleged drunken condition at the time Fagan carried out the attack, the
learned judge intimated that the recommendation would be forwarded to the proper quarters,
but warned Fagan not to build up much hope on mercy being shown before sentencing him to
death in the usual manner.

21

THE DRUNKEN HUSBAND

Joseph Fletcher, 15 December 1911

Even though he was very drunk, 40-year-old Joseph Fletcher realised immediately what he
had done. This time he had gone too far and knew that there would be dire consequences.

Surveying the scene, he put on his coat and, leaving his home on Bostock Street, Everton, he sought out a police officer. It was late on Saturday night, 2 September 1911, and as Fletcher headed towards Scotland Road, he decided on what tale he would tell to explain his actions.

PC James Rawson was patrolling his beat when he was summoned by Fletcher who told the officer that he needed help, as his wife had fallen down the stairs. They returned to the house and the constable could see that Caroline Fletcher lay unconscious at the foot of the stairs. It was also apparent, even from just a cursory glance, that her injuries were not consistent with such a fall. He summoned help and soon detectives began to quiz Fletcher's children who were all present in the house.

The two eldest, 17-year-old Catherine, and John, two years her junior, quickly dismissed their father's account of what had happened. Instead, they told detectives that Joseph Fletcher was a brute of a father who habitually beat his wife on the slightest pretext, but usually when he was drunk which, they added, was often. Catherine said that earlier that day, shortly after noon, Fletcher had arrived home from work and sent her to the shop for some cheese and beer for his lunch.

Finishing the beer, Fletcher then went out to the pub, and had been seen there, drinking constantly, since the early afternoon. At 9.30 p.m. their mother sent Catherine to fetch her father and when he failed to return as promised within ten minutes, she then sent her son John to bring him back.

Fletcher finally returned around 10.30 p.m. and was clearly very drunk. No sooner had he returned than he shouted for Catherine to go back to the pub and fetch him more beer. Caroline told her husband that he had had enough and they began to quarrel. She knew from past experience that it was unwise to get into a quarrel when he was in this state and so she sent the children to bed and prepared to follow them upstairs. Fletcher staggered towards the door and insisted that if no one would fetch him more beer he would go himself.

Drunken wife killer Joseph Fletcher.
(*T.J. Leech Archive*)

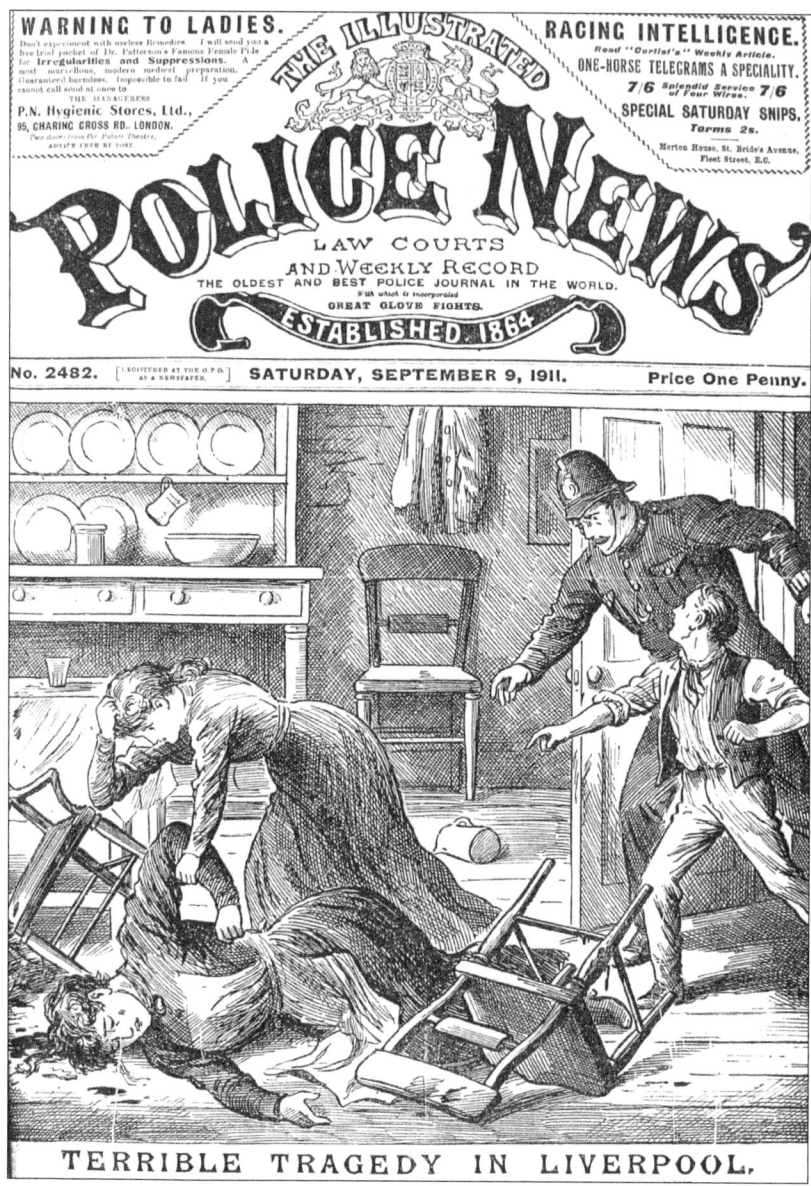

Fletcher's brutal crime was featured in the *Illustrated Police News*. (*T.J. Leech Archive*)

As soon as he set foot outside, Caroline went to the door and bolted it shut. Fletcher was still on the doorstep when he heard the bolt draw and began kicking at the door, demanding to be let back in. She reluctantly slid back the bolt and dashed back across the room as Fletcher stormed in, full of rage. Caroline went into the parlour and locked the door, only for Fletcher to kick it open. He went straight for his wife, punching and kicking her as the children stood by helplessly. He then picked up a chair and battered her over the head until she fell dead on the floor.

When he stood before Mr Justice Avory at Liverpool Assize on 11 November, his counsel attempted to show that he had been so incapacitated with drink as to be unaware of his actions. Tellingly, the story he had told the policeman, that his wife had fallen down the stairs, was used to suggest that no matter how drunk he may have been, he still had the presence of mind to realise he was in serious trouble and to fabricate a story to try to deflect the blame. Following conviction and the refusal of his appeal, Fletcher made an unsuccessful attempt to take his own life before becoming the seventh person to be executed that December by hangman John Ellis, in one of the busiest months for execution on record.

22

THE LIVERPOOL SACK MURDER

George Ball, 26 February 1914

At just after 7.30 p.m. on the evening of Wednesday 10 December 1913, and as a cold wind blew down Liverpool's Old Hall Street, ship's steward Walter Eaves was pacing up and down, waiting for his fiancée whom he had arranged to take to the cinema. As he passed Bradfield's sack and tarpaulin shop, a gust of wind caught hold of the wooden shutter on the shop front sending it toppling down, striking Eaves on the head.

Apart from the shock of the blow, Eaves was not injured, but the wooden shutter had damaged his derby hat, and when moments later, a young man hurried out from the shop to fix the shutter, Eaves berated him about the damage to the hat. The youth apologised and hurried back inside. Minutes later an older man came out, apologised for the accident and offered Eaves 2s to pay for the damage. Eaves accepted the money and moved a little farther down the street to continue his wait.

Five minutes later the younger man came out of the shop pushing a cart. Moments later the other man followed him outside, locked the door and Eaves watched as they headed off in the direction of Lock Fields and the Leeds and Liverpool Canal.

On the following morning, when typist Miss Venables arrived, she was shocked to find the shop had been opened by the two packers; 22-year-old George Sumner and 18-year-old Samuel Elltoft. There was no sign of the manageress, 40-year-old Christina Catherine Bradfield.

Miss Venables had left the warehouse at 6.40 p.m. on the previous evening, leaving Miss Bradfield alone with the two employees. When owner John Bradfield arrived a short time later, neither of the boys were able to help with the whereabouts of his sister, Christina. His suspicions were further heightened when Sumner claimed that Miss Bradfield had given him the keys to open up as she planned to be late in on the following day. Bradfield thought it highly unlikely that his sister would entrust the keys to staff and, when she had still not turned up by lunchtime, he contacted the police.

As Bradfield was speaking to a detective, across the city a barge master on the Leeds and Liverpool Canal discovered a strange bundle obstructing a lock gate. On closer examination it was discovered to be a heavy sack and fishing it out, it was found to contain the body of woman, trussed up with rope and weighted down by a large amount of scrap iron.

When detectives investigated the discovery, they found that the woman had been battered to death. Identification was soon complete when Bradfield recognised items found in the sack as belonging to the missing woman, and a visit to the mortuary confirmed the body was that of his sister.

When the discovery of the body was reported in the evening paper, Walter Eaves reported to the police the strange occurrence he had witnessed. Detectives at the shop found that money was missing and suspected an inside job. The statement made by Eaves seemed to confirm their theories and they decided to question again the two workers at their homes. Samuel Elltoft was picked up at his lodgings and taken into custody, but when officers went to pick up Sumner, they discovered his real name was George Ball, and that he was now missing. A search for the wanted man began in earnest. Bradfield put up a reward of £50 for information leading to his arrest. His photograph appeared frequently in newspapers and detectives were posted at railway stations and at the docks in case the fugitive tried to flee the area.

Ball was to be at liberty for eight days. On 20 December, his beloved Everton were playing Chelsea at Goodison Park and Ball was determined not to miss it. As he left the ground, he was recognised by a former neighbour who trailed him to a lodging house on Paradise Street, where he was arrested later that night.

Above left: Christina Bradfield. (*T.J. Leech Archive*)

Above right: Liverpool Sack Murderer, George Ball. (*T.J. Leech Archive*)

Ball and Elltoft were jointly tried before Mr Justice Atkin at Liverpool Assizes on 2 February 1914. Ball claimed he was innocent and that a stranger had burst into the shop while he was working in the warehouse. The man had pulled out a gun, threatening Miss Bradfield and when she refused to hand over the money in the till, he had clubbed her to death. He had then turned on Ball and threatened that he would also be shot if he didn't help the killer dispose of the body by dumping it in the canal. Ball said he had had no chance to escape and that he had been in fear of his life when he had helped with the removal of the body.

Under cross-examination, Ball's story collapsed. The prosecution claimed that Ball had had ample opportunity to escape from the killer, none more so than when he had gone outside to speak to Walter Eaves when the shutter had fallen on him. If Ball's version had been true, he could have simply asked Eaves to call the police. There was other evidence that suggested Ball was the killer. When arrested, he was in possession of a watch identified as belonging to Miss Bradfield and his landlord testified that on the day after the murder, Ball had had a significant amount of money, whereas on the day before, he had asked for a loan.

Elltoft claimed that he had not been present when the murder was committed and had only helped Ball to dispose of the body because he was scared Ball would implicate him if he refused. The jury took just a short time to find Ball guilty of murder and Elltoft guilty of a secondary charge of being an accessory.

Ball was sentenced to death but instead of being ushered from the dock, he was left to wait several minutes, staring around the court, as a sentence of four years was passed on his accomplice. Ball made a full confession while awaiting execution and a few days before his friend went to the gallows, Elltoft announced that he was to appeal against his sentence. On the following day, detectives went to his house where they recovered a quantity of money, hidden in the knob of a metal bedstead, and which was found to have been stolen on the night of the murder. With Elltoft facing a potential increase in sentence if he chose to appeal, and in light of the money discovered, he withdrew his appeal.

23

'THAT TERRIBLE THING'

Joseph Spooner, 14 May 1914

On Thursday 26 February 1914, less than three hours after George Ball had walked onto the scaffold inside Walton Gaol, a few miles across the city, a father and daughter were buying sweets in a small tobacconist shop on Upper Parliament Street. They walked out of the shop hand in hand and yet less than an hour later, the young girl was lying dead in the backyard of her house and a manhunt was on for her father.

Joseph Spooner, a 40-year-old labourer at the Liverpool docks, and his wife Catherine had separated in December 1913 following years of unhappiness and quarrelling due to his drinking. Taking their six children, Catherine had moved out of the marital home and had gone to stay with her sister on Oliver Street. In January 1914, with money tight and having received no financial help from her husband, she took out a summons against him for maintenance. The court ruled in her favour and she was granted an award of 12s a week. She then turned the screw tighter on Spooner by applying and winning a second summons against him for arrears in maintenance payments.

Following the break-up, Spooner had taken lodgings around the corner from Oliver Street, at 3 Upper Parliament Street. This allowed him easy access to his children, and he was a frequent visitor to the house as he tried to salvage his marriage. Spooner tried to keep up payments but soon fell in arrears and by the end of February, he had paid his wife a total of just 6s. Apart from the failure to make the payments, Catherine had also had enough of his drunken visits to the house, pleading for reconciliation and told him bluntly that they would never be together as a family again.

On Thursday 26 February, Spooner called at the house and asked to take the youngest daughter, Elizabeth for some sweets. They went off together towards the shop a few minutes walk from his house, where several witnesses, who knew both Spooner and his daughter well, including 9-year-old Grace Dutton, saw them walking and talking happily together.

At shortly after midday, Grace called at the Spooner house to play with the children. With the door unlocked, she let herself in and when she went out into the backyard she was horrified to find the body of little Elizabeth Spooner. Although still conscious, Elizabeth was bleeding badly from a horrific throat wound and was unable to speak. Lying beside her was the bag of sweets her father had purchased. She died a short time later.

The police were called and Joseph Spooner was arrested at his home soon after. At his trial before Mr Justice Bray at Liverpool Assizes on 24 April, his defence was insanity. His counsel made a dramatic plea that Spooner had no idea of what made him commit the crime, 'that terrible thing' he called it. Spooner also claimed that following an earlier separation, he had tried to commit suicide, as if this was testament to his weak state of mind, but his defence was rejected. The prosecution's case, that the crime was committed to extract revenge against his wife for her ending their relationship, was believed by the jury who took just a short time to find Spooner guilty as charged.

24

A BUCKET OF DIRTY WATER

Young Hill, 1 December 1915

The SS *Antillian* had set sail from New Orleans, USA, bound for England, on 6 July 1915. The ship was carrying a mixed cargo of general consumable goods and fuels, and in the holds below was a consignment of mules under the control of James Crawford. On the evening of Sunday 25 July, the ship docked at Bristol, where the mules were unloaded, before she continued on the last leg of the journey to Liverpool, arriving late on the following day.

At 7.30 p.m. on Monday 26 July, duty officer John Moore was on the bridge of the *Antillian* reading a book when he heard sounds of a disturbance. He looked up and saw Crawford running along the saloon deck towards the bridge with a horrific throat wound. Moore dropped his book and hurried down below onto the deck where he found Young Hill, a 28-year-old Louisiana Negro, holding a razor in his hand and threatening to kill anyone who approached him.

Moore notified the captain and chief officer who both armed themselves with revolvers and headed below. With Crawford already confirmed dead, and realising his position was hopeless, Hill meekly put down the razor and allowed himself to be placed under arrest.

When Hill stood trial at Liverpool Assizes before Mr Justice Ridley on 29 October, the events leading up to the murder were explained. It appeared that Crawford had been killed following a quarrel over a bucket of water. A seaman named Crockett had been off duty for several days and recuperating in his bunk when he had asked Hill for some water. Fellow sailors below deck later testified that Hill had offered him some water from a bucket, to which Crawford had objected. They began to quarrel, at which Hill grabbed Crawford's head, and forcing it back, drew his razor across his throat.

Hill admitted that they had quarrelled about conditions in the hold but claimed that he had told Crawford that he only wished to help the sick man and to make sure the water was clean. He said that Crawford had moved towards him aggressively, pulling something from his pocket, and thinking that it was a knife, Hill had acted in self-defence, withdrawing his razor and using it on his assailant.

However, the testimony of three fellow sailors, called as witnesses for the prosecution, supported the evidence that Hill had committed a brutal, unprovoked murder, and he was sentenced to death.

25

THE STALKER

John James Thornley, 1 December 1915

John Thornley had been courting Frances Johnson, a ring spinner in a Macclesfield cotton mill, for over two and a half years. At 26-years-old, two years older than his sweetheart, Thornley had yet to be called up for army service, and was working as a lamp man at Hibel Road railway station when their romance ended in the summer of 1915.

Frances had tired of the relationship after reaching the conclusion that they had hardly anything in common and little hope of a happy future together. Thornley seemingly chose to ignore her when she told him their relationship was over. He continued to call at Frances's house until her father warned him off. Frances had thus far treated the unwanted visits as nothing more than a nuisance, and there was nothing in Thornley's manner to suggest that anything unpleasant would result from them.

In September her parents went on holiday to Cleethorpes, leaving Frances alone at the house and she invited her neighbour May Warren to stay some nights with her. Thornley learned that her parents were away and began to stalk the girls. Night after night he took to following them from a distance, but they simply ignored him and after four days he gave up and left them alone.

On the evening of Friday 18 September, the girls visited a local theatre and by chance, bumped into Thornley. He followed them inside but took a seat some distance away and made no further contact with them. The girls returned home in the early hours and Frances locked all the doors, prepared a fire and breakfast for the morning and set her alarm clock. May Warren recorded what happened next:

> I was awoken at about 2.30am in the morning. I heard a bang in the yard. My first thoughts were that someone was trying to break in, so I listened quietly. Next I heard the rattle of a window as though someone had succeeded in forcing it, and then my alarm increased as I heard footsteps inside the house. My fears were confirmed when I heard someone knock against a table in the darkness. Not a sound up to this time had come from the bedroom in which Frances lay. When I heard the handle on the kitchen door being lifted I tried to muster up my courage to go to warn Frances. Springing out of my bed, I got half-way along the landing when there was a crash and, glued to the spot for a few seconds with fear, I made out the dark form of a man on the stairs.

Frances was found lying dead in her bed, with a shoemaker's knife placed in her left hand as if to suggest suicide. It was soon clear from medical examination that it had been placed after rigor mortis had set in, which discounted suicide and suggested murder. A letter found in the house led police to Thornley who was arrested the following Sunday morning.

Thornley's trial took place at Chester Assizes on Monday 25 October before Lord Coleridge. With all the evidence suggesting that Thornley had committed the brutal murder, the defence offered a plea of insanity. Doctors at Walton Gaol, who had observed Thornley while on remand, disputed this. Neither of them could find any signs of insanity or homicidal mania in the prisoner; there wasn't anything written in the letters or the way he had committed the murder to suggest insanity. Both spoke from vast experience of previous murderers and insanity.

Lord Coleridge, in his summing up, advised the jury to take into account evidence of the prisoner's mental state, but also reminded them that the murder weapon had been placed in Frances' left hand. Was this done to suggest that Frances' wounds were self-inflicted? Medical evidence had already ruled out this possibility, so was it an attempt by Thornley to shift the blame elsewhere? This would give a sure guide as to whether he knew right from wrong. The jury needed just fifteen minutes to find Thornley guilty as charged. There was no recommendation to mercy and the whole proceeding took just six hours.

Under normal circumstances, Thornley would have been hanged at Knutsford Gaol, which, at the turn of the last century, had taken over from Chester Castle as the execution site for murders committed in Cheshire. However, by the summer of 1915, Knutsford Gaol had been taken over by the military and no longer sanctioned executions. Thornley was therefore transferred to Walton Gaol for execution. It was not without incident.

Sharing the gallows with the Macclesfield murderer was American Negro sailor Young Hill (see chapter 24). Thornley had awaited his execution stoically and as the day drew closer, he told his guards that he knew hangman Ellis. 'I saw him in Manchester once. I expect he will be the one to do me in.'

At 9 a.m. on Tuesday 1 December, the two condemned men were led to the gallows. As Ellis strapped Thornley's wrists, he couldn't fail to see the tattoo on his forearm. It was a large red heart with the name 'Frances' boldly picked out. Thornley took his place on the drop and with the hood placed over his head and noose around his neck, he waited while Hill was made ready. As the American was noosed, he let out a fearful scream and began pleading to be spared. Unable to see what was happening, Thornley stood calmly until the trapdoors crashed down and Frances Johnson was avenged.

UNMOVED BY DEATH SENTENCE.

MACCLESFIELD MURDER CASE AT ASSIZES.

Unsuccessful Plea of Insanity.

Tragedy of Disappointed Love.

SELFISHNESS AS "CRUEL AS THE GRAVE."

[BY OUR OWN REPORTER.]

"May God Almighty have mercy on your soul!"

Slowly, and with impressive solemnity, Lord Coleridge, the Judge of Assize at Chester, on Wednesday afternoon pronounced the dread formula of judgment of death upon John James Thornley, railway lampman, 2

Newspaper cutting on the Macclesfield murder. (*T.J. Leech Archive*)

John James Thornley. (*Author's collection*)

26

ENTANGLEMENT

William Thomas Hodgson, 16 August 1917

My Dearest Helena,
Darling, I am worried to death about you because I think your mother mistrusts me. I shall not
leave you in the cold, and if you have the patience to wait until after Easter we will make some
arrangements, so don't worry. You will be all right with me before very long, and then I think we
shall both be satisfied, and your mother too.
From your ever loving boy,
Tom.

(Letter written by Tom Hodgson, April 1917)

Huddersfield-born 34-year-old William 'Tom' Hodgson had a guilty secret. Although he lived outwardly as loving husband and father with his wife, son and daughter on Central Park Avenue, Liscard, Cheshire, the silk buyer for a Birkenhead drapery firm was carrying on a relationship with a young waitress, an affair that had begun the week after Easter 1916.

Hodgson had moved to Liscard in 1915, finding work with Messrs. Robb Bros., and he soon made the acquaintance of Helena Llewellyn, a pretty young waitress who worked at the café close to his office. He asked her out, she accepted and they began a clandestine relationship. In March 1917, Helena discovered she was pregnant.

Hodgson assured her that he would 'do right' by her and reaffirmed this in a letter, asking her to be patient until 'after Easter' when he would make the appropriate arrangements. Early on the morning of 16 April, a neighbour heard raised voices from the Hodgsons' back kitchen. She heard Hodgson's daughter, Margaret shout 'Don't do that!' followed by her mother cry out.

There were no further sounds from the house except for the intermittent crying of the baby son in his cot upstairs. The crying went on throughout the afternoon, and at 6 p.m., the concerned neighbour went to investigate.

There was no answer to her knocking so she let herself in and discovered the bloodied bodies of Mrs Margaret Hodgson and three-year-old Margaret. They had been battered to death by the bloodstained hatchet that lay between their bodies. Detectives found no signs of a break-in or forced entry although it appeared that someone had tried to make it seem as though robbery was the motive: an empty purse lay on the table alongside an empty money box and in the front sitting room. a large portmanteau was packed with various items of silver, including a tea-pot and a new set of tea-knives.

Hodgson arrived home at 7.30 p.m. to find his house swarming with police. Neighbours also stood on the street watching events with a grim fascination.

'What's up here?' Hodgson asked the policeman at the door, forcing his way inside. No sooner had he entered than Hodgson pointed to the suitcase in the sitting room and shouted; 'Looks like something's wrong here, that's not mine!' He did the same with the bloodstained axe which had been moved to the table and pointed out that it wasn't his. At that point, Hodgson had not been informed of the murder of his wife and child but officers at the scene

Above left: Tom Hodgson. (*T.J. Leech Archive*)

Above right: Hodgson's home on Central Park Avenue, Liscard. (*Author's collection*)

were convinced that the seemingly distraught husband had expected to find the bodies of his wife and child. This quickly led to him becoming the main suspect and later that night Hodgson was arrested for the murder of his wife and angry neighbours hissed at him as he was led away by police.

He stood trial before Mr Justice Avory at Chester Assizes on 11 July 1917. Helena Llewelyn gave evidence on the second day of the trial. She told the court how she had met Hodgson the previous year and was unaware he was married with two children. In March 1917, on learning she was pregnant, he promised to do the right thing by her, both verbally and in writing, and the 'Dear Helena' letter was then read out aloud in court. The prosecution claimed he had committed the murder to release himself from the entanglement he had found himself in.

Hodgson denied that the arrangements planned involved killing his wife and child. Asked to explain how bloodstains came to be on his clothes, Hodgson said that he had cut himself shaving on the day of the murder, and forensic evidence was unable to prove whether this was true. Hodgson showed a total disregard for Helena Llewelyn's feelings by stating emphatically in court that he had never loved her, had no intentions of marrying her and even repudiated that he was the father of her illegitimate child. 'I had already tired of her by Christmas', he stated.

Hodgson may have spoken coldly of his affair to convince the jury that he had planned no ill for his wife and child, but his cold-hearted adultery did not help his cause. His counsel closed by asking the jury: 'Could this man really possess such a nerve as to murder his wife and child, go to work and about his business as usual, then calmly return home?'

They took a little under fifteen minutes to decide that he could and Hodgson showed no emotion as Mr Justice Avory sentenced him to death.

27

THE MAN WHO CAME BACK FROM THE DEAD

John Crossland, 22 July 1919

Twenty-nine-year-old John Crossland was proud to take the King's shilling in the summer of 1914 when the First World War broke out. Leaving his wife of eleven years, Ellen, and their four children at their home in Blackburn, he joined the British Expeditionary Force and was soon plunged straight into the hell of trench warfare. Within weeks, the battle of Mons took place in Belgium and Crossland was in the front line were he was caught up in an explosion and was believed to have been killed. When the fighting subsided, his comrades went to collect the dead for burial and Crossland was carried off the battlefield, thought to have been killed in action. It was only when a medic noticed signs of life that Crossland was rushed into the medical centre where his life was saved.

With the war at an end, Crossland was back in Blackburn living on Prince Albert Street, working as a labourer. The end of the war, in many ways, also signalled the end of the Crossland marriage. He left the family home, leaving Ellen with the four children: 15-year-old Selina; Joseph, aged 13; 10-year-old Evelyn; and Harold, aged 9. Ellen took out a maintenance order against her husband and when he fell behind with payments, he was sentenced to two months in prison.

Crossland was released from custody in March 1919, and attempted a reconciliation with his wife. All seemed well when he moved back into the family home, but within weeks, they began to quarrel again. This time the arguments stemmed from rumours Crossland had heard that while he had been inside that his wife had been 'carrying on' with another man. There was nothing to suggest this was true, and Ellen strenuously denied the allegations, but it created such tension that on Friday 2 May, Ellen asked the police to remove her husband from the house. Since the maintenance order was still active, officers called at the house and escorted Crossland from the premises.

Crossland was still convinced of his wife's infidelity and thus maintained that her lover, alleged to be a local man named William Kitchen, should now shoulder financial responsibility, and believed that he should no longer be bound by the order. He even went as far as serving his wife with a summons revoking the maintenance order. When this was met with no success, he decided to take the law into his own hands.

Early on the morning of Thursday 8 May 1919, Selina Crossland left the house to go to work and was shocked to find her father standing on the doorstep. He told her he had come to collect his army papers, as he planned to re-enlist, and Selina left the door open for him to enter as she made her way to work. Crossland climbed the stairs and entered the one bedroom where all the family slept. Crossland woke his wife and asked her for his army papers. She told him that she had destroyed them and asked him to leave. Crossland flew into a rage and strangled her. The disturbance awoke Joseph but his father assured him that everything was alright and together they went downstairs.

Crossland left the house and when Joseph went back upstairs to rouse his mother, he was horrified to find he was unable to wake her. The police were called and they found that she was dead and the cause of death was strangulation. On the following evening with a police searching for him, Crossland walked into Blackburn police station and surrendered.

When he stood trial before Mr Justice Salter at Liverpool Assizes on 30 June, Crossland pleaded guilty to manslaughter on the grounds of provocation, because Ellen had told him that she destroyed his army papers. The court heard that two days before she died, witnesses had heard Crossland make threats against her life. The train of events that morning were debated. Crossland said that he had entered the house as Selina had testified, and that failing to find his army papers in the downstairs bureau, he had gone upstairs and spoke to his wife, asking where they were. He said she told him she had burned them and they began to quarrel, during which time she fell and banged her head.

The jury found that Crossland had deliberately murdered his wife, and in returning a guilty verdict, added a recommendation for mercy. Mr Justice Salter told the Home Secretary that he did not concur with the recommendation to mercy. Crossland opted not to appeal and the man who had come back from the dead was hanged just three weeks after conviction.

28

SUICIDE PACT

Herbert Edward Rawson Salisbury, 11 May 1920

At the outbreak of the First World War, patriotic 35-year-old Bert Salisbury decided that his country needed him and, leaving his wife and family in America, to where they had emigrated from Formby at the turn of the century, he enlisted and was sent to France. Injured by flying shrapnel as the war entered its latter months, he was shipped home from the front line to a hospital in Leeds and into the care of a 38-year-old nurse, Alice Pearson. There was an instant attraction between the two, so much so that when Salisbury recovered from his injury and was discharged, he invited her to join him on a recuperation holiday.

With his wife and family in America, Salisbury saw himself as a single man. Alice Pearson was also married to a soldier serving in France, but despite this, she agreed to his request and they soon embarked upon a passionate affair. When Mark Pearson returned home in the spring of 1919, he discovered his wife's adultery and applied for a divorce, citing Salisbury as correspondent.

Once the divorce was finalised, Salisbury and Alice Pearson moved across the Pennines and took rented rooms in Southport, telling the landlord they were man and wife. Like many returning servicemen, Salisbury found work hard to come by and they were forced to live on Alice's savings which, although was a considerable amount, over £600, was soon being eaten away.

Shortly before 8 p.m. on the evening of Sunday 21 March 1920, Salisbury walked alone into the Blundell Arms public house at Formby, and ordered a whiskey and soda. He sat with his drink at the bar and at one point, accused the barman of staring at him. He slid off his bar stool and prepared to square up to the barman when John Clayton, a customer in the bar, spotted a revolver nestled in his waistband, and warned the barman from getting involved.

FORMBY MURDERER

PAYS PENALTY AT WALTON THIS MORNING.

OLDHAM MAN ALSO EXECUTED.

On the scaffold at Walton Gaol, this morning, Herbert Edward Rowson Salisbury and William Waddington suffered the last dread penalty of the law, fulfilling the old Mosaic injunction, which commands: "An eye for an eye and a tooth for a tooth."

Both criminals in the first double execution at Walton for some years are ex-soldiers who were wounded at the front.

Salisbury, who is a native of Formby, was the man who shot Alice Pearson, the divorced Leeds woman, with whom he had been living at Altcar. Having exhausted their money the two agreed to die together, and Salisbury has ever since shown by his actions and words his desire to complete the compact and rejoin his companion beyond the grave.

At police court and assize he proclaimed his guilt, declaring to his legal advisers, "I want to die. I have nothing to live for now." That determination, it is stated, never faltered to the last.

William Waddington, an Oldham piecer, was guilty of the brutal murder and outrage in that town of little Ivy Woolfenden, a girl only

Above left: Bert Salisbury. (*T.J. Leech Archive*)

Above right: Alice Pearson, shot dead by Bert Salisbury. (*T.J. Leech Archive*)

Left: Newspaper cutting relating to the Formby murder. (*T.J. Leech Archive*)

At closing time, Salisbury stumbled out of the door and slipped on the floor, bursting his nose in the fall. Clayton helped him to his feet and as he tried to stem the flow of blood from Salisbury's nose, the man pulled out his gun and said he had put four bullets into his 'wife'. Salisbury then began to run along the street, only for Clayton to chase after him and detain him until the police could be summoned. He was initially charged with being drunk and disorderly, but when officers interviewed him on the following morning, he confessed he had killed Alice Pearson and told them they would find her lying on the banks of the River Alt. Officers soon confirmed this was the case. Alice Pearson was discovered lying on the riverbank, covered in blood with four bullet wounds to the temple.

Salisbury pleaded guilty at his Liverpool Assizes trial before Mr Justice McCardie on 22 April. Following his arrest, he had made a statement to the effect that he and Alice had made a suicide pact, agreeing to live on her money until it was all gone, then he would kill her and then himself. On the night of the murder, they were down to their last £5 and decided it was time to stick to their agreement. The only problem was that while Mrs Pearson seemed to have gone along with her side of the agreement, Salisbury had certainly not.

The judge refused to accept his guilty plea and Salisbury's counsel offered a defence of insanity, based on him being too drunk at the time of the murder to be aware of what he was doing. After just a few minutes' deliberation, the jury rejected the insanity defence and found him guilty as charged.

Salisbury refused to appeal and, although a petition was raised asking for a reprieve, the prisoner told his solicitor he hoped it would be ignored as he wished to keep his side of the agreement he had made with Alice Pearson.

29

THE VALENTINE'S DAY MURDER

William Waddington, 11 May 1920

On the afternoon of Saturday 14 February 1920, 7-year-old Ivy Woolfenden called into a grocer's shop on Higginshaw Road, Oldham and asked for a sixpence to be changed into pennies, telling the shopkeeper that one of them was for her.

A few minutes earlier, Iris' sister Doris had been playing in the street with her friend, Elizabeth Roberts when Elizabeth's uncle, William Waddington shouted for them to fetch Doris' sister as he wanted her to run an errand. Ivy was initially reluctant to go but the promise of a penny was enough for her to change her mind.

Thirty-four-year-old William Waddington had fought bravely in both the Manchester and King's Liverpool Regiments during the First World War, and had been wounded in action three times. He was discharged following the Armistice but returning to his home in Royton, near Oldham, he had been unable to find regular work and had re-enlisted, only to desert his

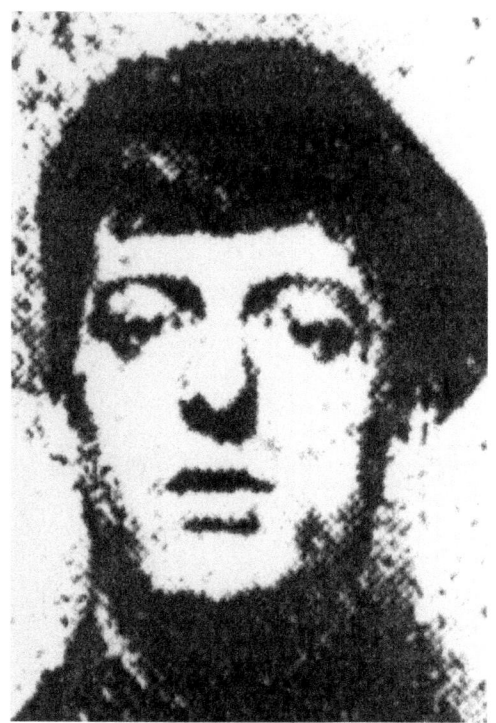

Above left: Ivy Woolfenden.
(*T.J. Leech Archive*)

Above right: Child-killer William
Waddington. (*T.J. Leech Archive*)

Left: Letter confirming
the planned execution of
Waddington. (*Author's collection*)

Any communication on the
subject of this letter should be
addressed to :—
THE UNDER SECRETARY OF STATE,
HOME OFFICE,
LONDON, S.W. 1,
and the following number quoted :—
403128/6.

HOME OFFICE,
WHITEHALL.

7th May, 1920.

Sir,

    I am directed by the Secretary of State to acquaint you
that, having had under his consideration the case of
William Waddington, now lying under sentence of death
in Liverpool Prison, he has failed to discover any
sufficient ground to justify him in advising His Majesty
to interfere with the due course of law.

       I am,

         Sir,

         Your obedient Servant,

         E Blackwell

The Chairman of
    the Prison Commissioners.

regiment when he found being a peacetime soldier was not to his liking. He returned home and found a position as a spinner at Monarch Mill in nearby Royton.

When Ivy returned from the errand, she was seen entering Waddington's house, a large three-storey end terrace at 192 Edge Lane Road, Higginshaw. She was never seen again. A short time later, Waddington left the house and locked the door behind him, giving Elizabeth Roberts the key. When she asked him where Ivy was, Waddington said he did not know and then headed off down the street.

Waddington's mother, Eliza arrived home from shopping at 4.30 p.m. Unable to get into the house, she went to her daughter Emma's house and together with another daughter they returned to the house and let themselves in. What they found were several bloodstains and they heard sounds of moaning coming from the cellar. They went down the stairs and were greeted with a pitiful sight. Ivy was lying face down on the cellar, her dress pulled up and her underclothes removed. She had been severely battered about the head, and although semi-conscious, she was making a pitiful moaning sound.

Mrs Waddington rushed outside and attracted the attention of a neighbour who went down to the cellar and carried the battered and bloodied body of Ivy Woolfenden upstairs and out of the house. An ambulance and police were summoned and a crowd gathered as the ambulance arrived. Before medical attention could be given, Ivy died from her injuries. Police officers arrived and found a bloodstained hammer, the likely murder weapon, on the cellar floor. Also found on the cellar floor was the bloodstained penny that Ivy had been given for going on the errand.

A manhunt began for the immediate suspect and Waddington was traced to Todmorden. He denied any knowledge of the crime and claimed to have been in Leeds that morning and had spent the time walking across the Pennines back to Todmorden. Officers knew he was lying as he was known to have been in work that morning and several witnesses, not least his niece, Elizabeth, gave evidence that she had seen him Oldham that lunchtime. He had bloodstains on his clothes and scratches on his hands and arms. He was hissed and booed as he was taken into custody.

When Waddington stood trial before Mr Justice McCardie at Liverpool Assizes on 21 April, the evidence against him was damning. As witness after witness entered the dock to give evidence, the noose tightened around the prisoner's neck. The defence had a hopeless task and put forward a plea of insanity caused by the injuries he had sustained fighting for his country.

Found guilty of murder, he was hanged alongside Bert Salisbury (see chapter 28) and they were buried in adjacent felons' graves that afternoon. The *Oldham Chronicle* summed up the crime perfectly saying that: 'Even in these times of hysteria and revolting crimes, Waddington's offence stands out as matching almost the worst.'

30

A FATAL SLIP-UP

James Ellor, 11 August 1920

James and Ada Ellor had married in July 1907. For Ada, it was her second marriage, having lost her first husband at an early age, and when James was called up at the outset of the First

H.M. Prison *Liverpool*

11 August 1920

Register No. *5925* Name *James Ellor*

GENTLEMEN,

As directed in Standing Order No. 577, I have the honour to submit the annexed Record of the execution of the above-named Prisoner, which took place at *8* o'clock on the morning of the *11th August 1920*

The Inquest was held on the same day, when the Jury returned the following verdict:—° "James Ellor died by his being hanged by the neck until dead within the walls of this H.M.Prison at Liverpool, in accordance with the law"

I am, Gentlemen,

Your obedient Servant,

To the
Prison Commissioners,

Above left: James Ellor.
(*T.J. Leech Archive*)

Above right: Ada Ellor.
(*T.J. Leech Archive*)

Left: Official notice of James Ellor's execution having been carried out.
(*T.J. Leech Archive*)

World War, she probably feared she might also lose another husband. Ellor initially joined the Cheshire Regiment and later, following a transfer to the Shropshire Light Infantry, he was gassed and wounded in an explosion. He spent some time at home on leave before rejoining his unit and in March 1918, Ada wrote to inform him that she was pregnant. By return, Ellor wrote a letter to his wife telling her that he had fallen in love with another woman and that she too was pregnant. A few days later, a second letter arrived, asking her to ignore the previous one, which had been sent by a friend as some sort of prank.

Following the Armistice, Ellor returned to their home in Hyde, Cheshire, finding work as a hat maker, but shortly thereafter, he took to drinking heavily. This put such a strain on their marriage that Ada had soon had enough. On 25 March 1920 she moved out of their home and took lodgings at 8 Travis Street, Hyde, and also took out a summons against him for cruelty.

On the following day, Ellor spoke to his stepson Harry Forbes, Ada's son from her first marriage, and begged him for Ada's new address. Forbes believed Ellor was genuinely apologetic and keen to save his marriage so he gave him the new address.

At 10.30 a.m. the following morning, James called at the house on Travis Street, and begged Ada for another chance. She refused and later that afternoon, Ellor approached a policeman and confessed that he had battered his wife to death with a hammer.

At Chester Assizes before Lord Chief Justice Coleridge on 6 July, Ellor stood on trial for his life. His counsel claimed first that the crime may well have been provoked through jealousy, hinting that Mrs Ellor was of loose character and had driven her husband to commit the crime.

When this was destroyed in court, they then sought to show that Ellor was insane and referred to his war record, claiming that the gas poisoning he had suffered still affected him. Ellor stated that he heard voices in his head and was often unaware of what he was doing. He had, however, made a fatal slip-up. On remand at Manchester's Strangeways Prison, Ellor had shared a cell with a prisoner named Joe Kearon and had confided in him that he had murdered his wife because she refused to take him back, and that his claim of hearing voices was a sham. Kearon gave evidence against him and helped send the brutal wife murderer to the gallows.

31

THE BUSINESS CARD

Frederick George Wood, 10 April 1923

Invalided out of the Northumberland Fusiliers in November 1917, Fred Wood had been granted a small army pension and, unable to find regular employment in his hometown of Bradford, he chose to seek his fortune on the road. To make ends meet, he travelled to Cheshire and gained employment as an upholsterer, staying in cheap lodgings and calling from door-to-door in search of work.

Wood's luck was in on the morning of Monday 18 December 1922, when he called at a house in Bramhall, Cheshire and was given the chance to earn some money. Ninety-five Acre Lane was a pleasant villa, set back off the road, and was the home of a 50-year-old spinster, Margaret Gilchrist White, and her brother John, a banking clerk who worked in Manchester.

Miss Gilchrist White had spoken to the postman at around 9.15 a.m. that morning, and two hours later, a neighbour had heard the sound of someone hammering from inside the house. A caller at 4.30 p.m. had received no reply.

John White arrived home at 7 p.m. and found the house ransacked and in darkness. Lighting the gas, he entered the dining room and discovered the body of his sister lying on her back with her hands tied together and resting against her throat. She was fully clothed although her apron had been pulled up to cover her face.

The police arrived and a search of the house revealed the contents of several drawers had been emptied on the floor and although a number of jewellery boxes had been forced open, it seemed that the killer was interested only in cash, as a gold watch and other items of jewellery lay untouched on the dressing table. The killer seemed to have made little effort to cover his tracks. There were clear fingerprint impressions on all of the items, and on the bedroom floor, completely out of place, was a length of webbing used to repair chairs.

There was no sign of a forced entry. John White told police that there was a chair in the hallway, which hadn't been there when he left for work. The chair had been stripped down for re-upholstering. This tied in with the piece of webbing found upstairs, suggesting the involvement of a furniture repairer, and the biggest clue left at the scene was a workman's business card.

The card gave the name: Fred Wood 'Upholsterer', c/o Mrs Cooper, Church Street, Wilmslow. Detectives travelled to Church Street only to be told that Wood had left the area several days earlier. They were given a good description of the wanted man, and posters were displayed outside police stations across the north of England.

Above left: Strangler Fred Wood. (*T.J. Leech Archive*)

Above right: Hangman John Ellis executed fourteen men on the gallows at Walton Gaol, including Fred Wood. (*Author's collection*)

Wood was described as a man possibly using the alias Ronald Lee; aged 29-years-old; 5ft 7in tall; clean shaven; last seen wearing a light tweed suit, light coloured cap, blue collar and tie, black army boots, gunshot wounds on his left arm; and tattoos on his arms and chest.

On the morning of Saturday 23 December, Wood walked into a police station at Lincoln. He admitted having done some work for Miss White but strenuously denied murdering her. His version of events was not convincing and he was charged with murder.

Wood subsequently stood trial before Mr Justice Rigby Swift at Chester Assizes on 1 March. Wood's counsel offered a defence that the death had been accidental and that Wood had stolen from the house to facilitate his escape, as he felt certain he would be blamed for what had happened. 'If the accused had intended to commit robbery, surely he would have stolen the watch and jewellery' his counsel told the jury.

Wood claimed that while he was repairing a chair, the woman had suffered a fit and had accidentally strangled herself. His counsel also suggested that Wood's war wound meant that he had little strength in his injured arm as to cause strangulation. This was countered by the prosecution who pointed out that Wood clearly had enough strength in his arm to get sufficient tension in the webbing when re-upholstering chairs.

The prosecution pointed to a clear motive for the murder by asking the jury: 'Do you know a greater motive for murder in the world than the greed of gold?'

The jury clearly agreed and took less than an hour to find Wood guilty of murder, adding a strong recommendation for mercy. An appeal before the Lord Chief Justice was heard, based on the fact that the trial judge didn't allow the jury to consider a verdict of manslaughter, but was quickly dismissed.

32

TORN BETWEEN TWO LOVERS

James Winstanley, 5 August 1925

Eighteen-year-old Edith 'Edie' Horrocks-Wilkinson was doing her bit for King and country,working in a Wigan munitions factory, when she first met James Winstanley. He was two years older than Edie and although they began a relationship, they seemed to spend most of their time quarrelling. Winstanley was working as a miner at Ellerbeck Colliery and was exempt from conscription and although they met up with other each other several times a week, it was hardly the great love affair she had imagined.

With the Armistice signed and the country getting back on its feet, Edie left the munitions works and took a job as a barmaid at the Black Horse on Elliot Street, Wigan. One of the regulars there was Harry Taylor, a handsome ex-soldier and she soon found herself falling in love. She broke off her romance with Winstanley and was delighted when, a few months later, she found herself pregnant. Taylor proposed marriage.

However, no sooner had he made the proposal than he changed his mind, telling Edie he wanted to wait a few years before settling down. Her parents were enraged at Taylor's refusal to wed and when Edie went against their wishes to continue seeing him, they told her to leave home, whereby she went to live with a relative.

In the spring of 1920, Edith gave birth to a daughter, also named Edith, and although refusing to marry Edie, Taylor nonetheless was eager to pay for the child's upbringing and contributed regular maintenance payments. They continued their relationship and while Edie still harboured hopes of their finally getting wed and having more children, unbeknown to her, Taylor was already making other plans.

The homeland for which Taylor had fought to preserve its freedom, and to which hero soldiers had been gloriously welcomed back, failed to be the land fit for heroes that the government had promised. Job opportunities were few and far between, and in Wigan, unemployment was as bad as anywhere. It came as some surprise when, in the summer of 1922, Taylor told Edie he had decided to try his luck in America, but would continue to provide for her and baby Edith, and when he was straight, he would send for them.

Once settled in America, Taylor, as promised, wrote regularly and sent money. But within a year, the letters and money stopped and sadly, she concluded that Taylor must have found someone else. It was while she was still coming to terms with the shock of the apparent rejection that she became reacquainted with Winstanley when he happened into her bar one afternoon.

Winstanley had just lost his job and was equally depressed, and they began to take comfort in each other. Within weeks they had become lovers again and this time her feelings for him were much stronger than before. It seemed their old quarrelling days were behind them and they even began to discuss their future when, out of the blue, in April 1924, on Edith's 26th birthday, a letter arrived from America.

Taylor wrote to her saying that he had managed to set himself up in business and enclosed money for the passage to America for Edie and the child. Edie decided to accept the offer of a new life in America and told Winstanley, for the second time that their relationship was over.

It was then that fate dealt a cruel hand. Like England, America was also going through a depression and with work getting scarcer to find, one of the first things put into place was a temporary restriction on immigration.

With Edie's trip put on hold, Winstanley was not about to let her go for a second time without a fight. Delighted at the news of the postponed sailing, he worked hard at saving the relationship to the extent that when the American immigration laws were later relaxed, Edie began to find reasons of her own to delay her departure. She was literally now torn between two lovers.

On 7 May 1925, Edith and Winstanley spent the night drinking in several pubs at Gathurst and were last seen leaving the Navigation walking hand in hand along the canal bank. Later that night, Winstanley returned to his home on Warrington Road, Goose Green alone and told his sister that he had strangled Edith. He led police officers to a wood beside the canal where he pointed out her body in the undergrowth.

At his trial before Mr Justice Fraser, beginning on 18 June 1925, the prosecution claimed that Winstanley had deliberately raped and strangled her, because she had told him earlier that evening she had made up her mind to go to America.

Winstanley's two-fold defence was weak. His counsel claimed that the couple enjoyed inflicting pain on each other during sex and that he had strangled her accidentally as they had made love, with her consent. They also claimed he was insane and that the sadistic nature of the crime supported this.

On the second day of the trial, the jury needed just a short time to return a guilty verdict and although over 20,000 people signed a petition for Winstanley's reprieve, it was not to be. He spent his last night on earth making jigsaws in the condemned cell, singing a popular song of the time, 'Only one more night to roam'. According to hangman Willis, who was carrying out his 106th execution, Winstanley was 'a smart chap with a strong muscular neck. Walked as firm as a rock. No trouble. Death inst.'

Above left: Edie Horrocks. (*T.J. Leech Archive*)

Above right: James Winstanley. (*T.J. Leech Archive*)

The towpath at Gahurst, close to where Edie Horrocks was brutally murdered. (*Author's collection*)

Above left: Hangman William Willis. (*Author's collection*)

Above right: Winstanley leaves court after being sentenced to death. (*T.J. Leech Archive*)

33

'WHAT THE LAW ORDERS'

Lock Ah Tam, 23 March 1926

'*Send your folks please, I have killed my wife and child!*'
(Telephone call made by Lock Ah Tam, 2 December 1925)

The man sounded highly agitated and spoke in an accent that was Oriental with a faint trace of the local 'Scouse' accent. After stammering for a few seconds, he then said something that had police officers hurrying to the house at 122 Price Street, Birkenhead. It was the early hours of Wednesday 2 December 1925, and when detectives reached the house, they found the tragic end to a story that had roots stretching back since the latter days of the First World War.

The caller had identified himself as 54-year-old Lock Ah Tam, a Chinese-born former seaman. Tam was born in Canton in 1872 and worked as a sailor onboard ships that regularly travelled to Liverpool. At the age of 25, he decided to stay in the port and found a job working as a shipping office clerk. His wife Catherine, a Welsh-born woman soon bore him four children, although one died in infancy, and with his ability to speak good English as well as his native tongue, he became a popular member of the Chinese community, often acting as an interpreter if any of his fellow countrymen found themselves in trouble.

He founded the Chinese Republic Progress Club on Liverpool's Pitt Street in the heart of the Chinese community, which offered hospitality for visiting Chinese seamen. It was here in August 1918, when Tam tried to mediate in a dispute between groups of Chinese and drunken Russian sailors that he received a blow to the head from a billiard cue.

From then on, he became prone to violent mood swings and took to drinking heavily. His family also bore the brunt of his change in temperament, and following one particularly fearsome rant against his son Lock Ling, Tam realised it would be for the boy's benefit to go to school in China and arranged for relatives in Canton to look after his son until he returned to Liverpool.

The change in behaviour had an adverse effect on his business. A shipping venture he had heavily invested in collapsed, resulting in him losing £10,000, and by 1924, he was declared bankrupt.

At the end of November 1925, Lock Ling returned from China. The years away from home had seen him grow into an independent young man and one afternoon, when at the family house, his father chastised him for letting the fire go out, Lock Ling simply told him 'I'm not here to put the coal on the fire.' Lock Ah Tam was also having constant run-ins with his son over the late hours he was keeping. Despite all this, Tuesday 1 December 1925 was his son's 21st birthday and Tam organised a family party.

There were over a dozen guests at the gathering and Tam was seen to be in good spirits, offering the traditional Chinese toast of *fat choy* (long life) to his son. The party broke up around midnight by which time Tam had drunk a considerable amount.

The family retired to bed, only for the children to be woken by shouting from their parents' bedroom downstairs. Lock Ling dressed and went to investigate whereby he found his parents having a quarrel. The two daughters had also dressed and gone downstairs. Seeing their father clearly enraged, Lock Ling told the women to stay in the kitchen while he went next door to speak to neighbour Kwok Taan Chin, whom he felt would be able to calm his father down.

During the next few minutes, chaos broke out. Tam took out a gun and began to fire it. The women cowered in the kitchen while Ling rushed to find a policeman. Tam was able to force the kitchen door and fired a number of shots, killing his wife and youngest daughter, Cecilia, instantly, and fatally wounding their other daughter, Doris, who would die from her injuries a month later. After making the telephone call to the police, Tam sat in the parlour, calmly smoking a cigarette, waiting for the police to take him away.

 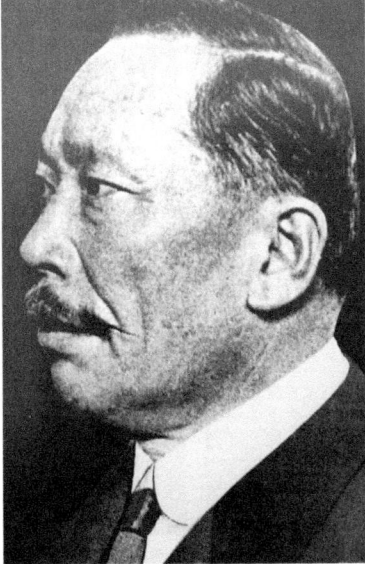

Right: Doris Tam, shot dead by her father. (*T.J. Leech Archive*)

Far right: Lock Ah Tam. (*Author's collection*)

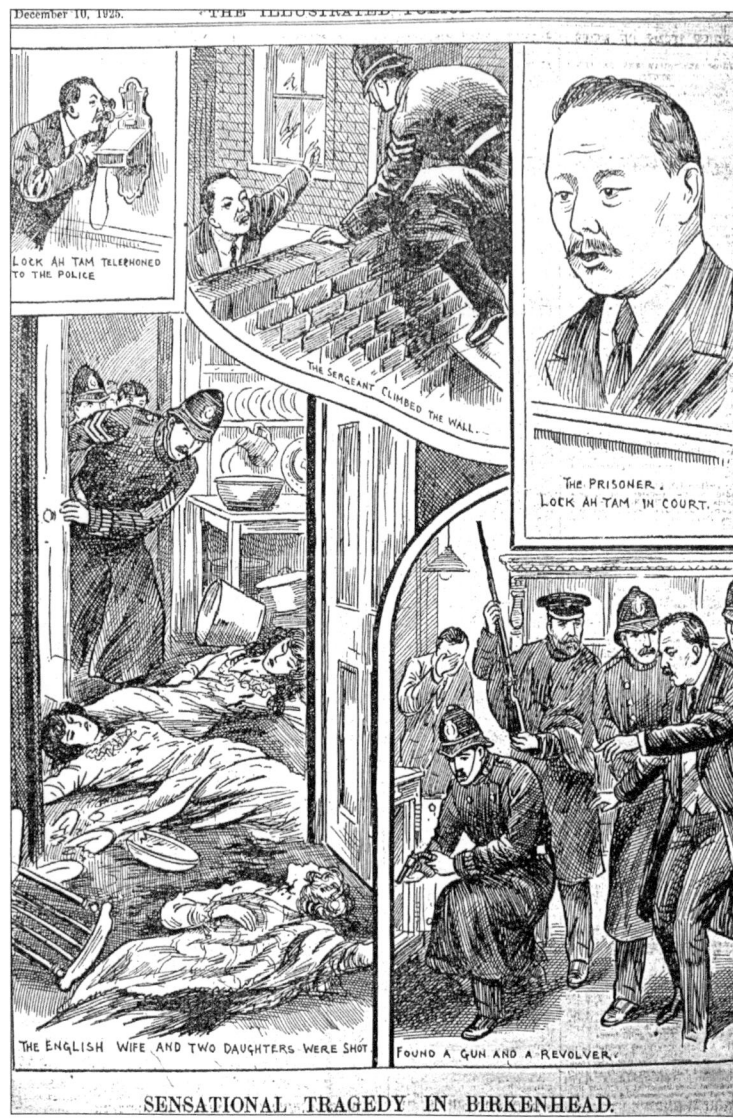

Lock Ah Tam's murder
as recorded in the
Illustrated Police News.
(*T.J. Leech Archive*)

At his trial before Mr Justice Mackinnon at Chester Assizes on 5 February 1926, Tam's defence was that he was insane. There was ample medical evidence to show that he had many signs of insanity, violent mood swings and an uncontrollable temper, but the most telling thing against him was the phone call he had made to the police, which suggested that he was conscious of what he had done, and crucially, that it was wrong.

As this fell outside the scope of the McNaughten Rules, the archaic guidelines used to assess if a person was insane or not, the defence of insanity failed and it took the jury just twelve minutes to return their guilty verdict.

As he waited to be hanged, Tam wrote a letter of thanks to his solicitor, stating that he knew now that what he did was wrong, although he didn't at the time. 'If I have done wrong, however, they must do with me what the law orders them to do.'

34

'MY BEST GIRL'

James Leah, 16 November 1926

James Leah was a giant of a man. An imposing figure with a thick black beard, even in his 60th year, he was still a hard-working farmer running Finlow Farm, at Over Alderley, near Wilmslow. He was, however, quick-tempered and over-bearing and had taken to drinking many years before. As a result, his wife of forty-two years had left him many times on account of his bullying and drunkenness, and on one occasion, twenty years before, she had applied for a separation order, although she had subsequently returned to the family after just a few weeks away. They had twelve children, although by the summer of 1926, only three remained at home – Louise, Elsie and John – each of whom had learned to live in the turbulent, quarrelsome environment.

By the autumn of 1926, the atmosphere at Finlow Farm had become so unbearable that on 9 September, young John Leah told his father he was leaving. Matters had come to a head due to Leah's unreasonable conduct regarding the two men who were courting both Louise and Elsie. He refused to allow them to visit the house and was rude and aggressive to them whenever he saw them outside the house.

Mrs Leah and the two remaining daughters decided that enough was enough and also made secret plans to leave the farm for good. On Friday 24 September, the family ate breakfast together before Mrs Leah packed her bags and went to stay on neighbouring Dickens Farm, run by her daughter and son-in-law.

When Leah realised his wife had left him, he asked Louise where she had gone. Upon being told where, he lost his temper and when the quarrel escalated, the elder daughter Elsie said that she too intended to move out that day, and shortly after lunchtime, she called a taxi.

With Elsie gone 20-year-old Louise, his favourite daughter, tried to placate her father. Leah was enraged and a short time later Louise staggered across the field to Dickens Farm, with blood gushing from deep cuts to her neck. She collapsed on the kitchen floor and died a short time later.

The police were quickly called to Finlow Farm and found James Leah, lying with a self-inflicted neck injury in a fodder bin. Leah was able to make a statement regarding the attack, claiming: 'I did her in the kitchen. I cut myself with this knife and came here to finish it off. She's my best girl. I couldn't bear her to go. My poor Louise.'

Leah's trial before Mr Justice Fraser at Chester Assizes on Wednesday 17 October was a formality. His counsel realised the futility of trying to show that Leah had not killed his daughter, and concentrated on securing a verdict of manslaughter. Leah made for a pathetic figure in the dock, speaking quietly and admitting that he had killed Louise because she had also told him she planned to move out of the farm that afternoon.

'Don't go, Louie, stay here with me, I pleaded with her' he told the court and that after she had answered him back snappily, he lost his temper. Leah then broke down, as did many people in the visitor's gallery.

The prosecution simply claimed that no matter how sad the facts behind the case were, it was simply one of wilful murder and that Leah had a violent temper and had often in the past flown into a rage with his family. The jury took just one hour to consider their guilty verdict, but added a recommendation of mercy.

Finlow Farm, Over Adderley. (*Author's collection*)

Bloodstains on the floor of the farmhouse at Finlow Farm. (*Author's collection*)

ALDERLEY FARM CRIME.

— • —

Father Pays Penalty For Daughter's Murder.

— • —

James Leah (60), farmer, was executed at Walton Gaol, Liverpool, at eight o'clock on Tuesday morning for the murder of his daughter Louise, aged 20. The girl lived with her father at Finlow Farm, Over Alderley, and he became incensed because she threatened to leave. Injuries were inflicted with a hedge chopper on the girl's neck and head. Leah was found in a fodder bin with his throat cut, but he recovered in hospital.

The condemned man had been ill since being incarcerated at Walton Gaol, and had been an inmate of a hospital ward.

The chaplain of the prison sustained and cheered him up to Monday, but was prevented from attending him further owing to illness, and his place was taken by Captain J. Ford, a missioner, who consoled the condemned man and bade him farewell.

Newspaper cutting recording James Leah's execution. (*Author's collection*)

35

NO LUCK ANYWHERE

William Meynell Robertson, 6 December 1927

'I am going out. Stiffy is going to do for me and himself as well. There is no luck anywhere for him, try as he will, and I cannot help anymore. We have had this alternative for weeks. Tried everything, so it must be done.'

(Telegram sent by Eve Jennings to her brother, August 1927)

Jimmy Goddard was making his way home from work along a footpath adjacent to Dam Wood, Speke, when he was horrified to see a man emerge from the wood covered in blood. It was just after 6 p.m. on Monday 15 August 1927. With blood oozing from a gaping throat wound, the man was making a frightful gurgling sound and pointing to something inside the wood.

Goddard remembered seeing a policeman a few minutes earlier so he rushed back to alert him and soon both Goddard and the officer followed the man into the woods. As they made their way in, the man took out a piece of paper and pencil and scribbled: 'I loved her only but we could not live. Save her, not me.'

Inside the wood they discovered the body of a woman, lying on the grass, her throat cut so violently that her head was almost decapitated. The man, who was identified as William Robertson, a 32-year-old salesman, was rushed to hospital. At the hospital Robertson wrote a further note, explaining his actions. He wrote that the woman he had killed was Evelyn Mary Jennings, and that they had planned to commit suicide together in a pact.

The whole background to the case was told to the court when Robertson appeared before Mr Justice Acton at Liverpool Assizes on 28 October. The court heard that Robertson had served in the army throughout the war, both in the ranks and as a commissioned officer, until he was demobbed in November 1919.

In 1922 he had married but had never properly supported his wife who left him early in 1924. He had also been unable to hold down a job for any period of time. In August 1924 he became acquainted with a Miss Hall, the proprietress of a café in Liverpool. He had cohabited with her, then gambled all her money and ran off leaving her penniless, despite promises to marry her when he was divorced.

He had met 33-year-old Evelyn (Eve) Jennings two years earlier when she had worked in a hairdresser's close to the café run by Miss Hall. Robertson began an affair with her but was soon gambling all her money and pawning her property. By the summer of 1927, their luck was out and they were both penniless.

Earlier on the day of the murder, Eve had written a number of letters to relatives indicating that she and the prisoner had decided to die together, including a telegram to her brother that was read out in court.

Robertson's counsel tried in vain to plead insanity. In summing up, the judge agreed that the suicide pact was almost certainly true, but the fact remained that the prisoner had wilfully killed another person and the only verdict possible in this case was guilty of murder.

For a time it was touch and go whether the hangman's services would be required at all. In attempting to take his own life, Robertson had badly injured his own throat, leaving him

Particulars of the condemned Prisoner.	Particulars of the Execution.	Records respecting the Executioner and his Assistants (if any).	Name and Address, in full, of the Executioner.	Name and Address, in full, of the 1st Assistant to the Executioner (if any).	Name and Address, in full, of the 2nd Assistant to the Executioner (if any).
Name *William Meynell* ROBERTSON	The length of the drop, as determined before the execution. *5'* feet *11* 'inches.		*Thomas William Pierrepoint, Town End, Clayton, Bradford, Yorks*	*Thomas M. Phillips, 208 Aldar Road, Farnworth, Bolton, Lancs*	
Register Number *2358*	The length of the drop, as measured after the execution, from the level of the floor of the scaffold to the heels of the suspended culprit. *6'* feet ___ inches.				
Sex *Male*	Cause of death. [(a) Dislocation of vertebrae, (b) Asphyxia.]	Opinion of the Governor and Medical Officer as to the manner in which each of the above-named persons has performed his duty.			
Age *32*	(a) *Dislocation of vertebra*	1. Has he performed his duty satisfactorily?	1. *Yes*	1. *Yes*	1.
Height *5'.7½"*		2. Was his general demeanour satisfactory during the period that he was in the prison, and does he appear to be a respectable person?	2. *Yes*	2. *Yes*	2.
(Build) *Short & Strong.*	Approximate statement of the character and amount of destruction to the soft and bony structures of the neck.	3. Has he shown capacity, both physical and mental, for the duty, and general suitability for the post?	3. *Yes*	3. *Yes*	3.
	Separation of the spinal cord, between 2nd and 3rd cervical vertebrae	4. Is there any ground for supposing that he will bring discredit upon his office by levanting, or by giving interviews to persons who may seek to elicit information from him in regard to the execution or by any other act?	4. *No*	4. *No*	4.
	If there were any peculiarities in the build or condition of the prisoner, or in the structure of his neck, which necessitated a departure from the scale of drops, particulars should be stated.	5. Are you aware of any circumstances occurring before, at, or after the execution which tend to show that he is not a suitable person to employ on future occasions either on account of incapacity for performing the duty, or because of his creating public scandal before or after an execution?	5. *No*	5. *No*	5.
Weight in clothing (to be taken on the day preceding the execution)	*No.*				
Character of the prisoner's neck					

Robertson's execution was detailed in the LPC4 sheet which recorded every execution at the prison. (Author's collection)

with a freshly healed scar running across the front of his neck. Such an injury could result in the prisoner being decapitated following execution and more than one condemned man had been spared to prevent this. Dr Ahern, the medical officer at Walton examined the prisoner following conviction and believed that the injury had sufficiently healed and that he was fit enough to be executed; a hangman was notified that the execution was to go ahead.

Having observed the prisoner in his cell, Tom Pierrepoint took note of the neck injury and shortened the drop accordingly. It was noted on the official form that the execution was a success but when the drop fell, blood oozed from the scar and when the hangmen went to remove the body after it had been hanging for an hour, there was a large pool of blood on the floor.

36

'PLAYING THIS GAME FOR TOO LONG'

Albert George Absalom, 25 July 1928

Albert Absalom had left the army in 1923 after serving two and a half years and returned to Liverpool, taking lodgings at 474 Scotland Road. Absalom's health was not good and he did little work in the following years, but he had worked for a time as a labourer in a mill and it was here, shortly after his demob that he met Mary Alice Reed. They became engaged and began to plan for a future together, purchasing furniture and other items for when they got their own house.

Although they had been together for almost five years, due to Absalom's inability to hold down a regular job, Mary sensed that her hopes for an idyllic married life were no closer now than when they first met. She persuaded him to find work; he agreed and in the winter of 1927, he took the position of managing his brother-in-law's fish and chip shop.

By the spring of 1928, Absalom had started to become increasingly jealous of Mary's friendship with other men, both workmates and neighbours near her parents home on Garibaldi Street. She began to tire of Absalom's jealous rants and her feelings for him started to cool. Mary had been a regular visitor to the chip shop during the winter months but now that spring had arrived and the nights grew longer and lighter, her appearances became fewer and fewer.

This increased Absalom's feelings of jealousy and he began to suspect that she was having an affair. Events came to a head when she went out for the evening with neighbour William Cliffe. Cliffe had known Mary since school and on 4 May, when she got a puncture on her bicycle, he offered to repair it for her. With the bike now roadworthy, she accepted his suggestion to go out for a ride together and they spent several hours in each other's company.

That evening a customer told Absalom he had seen Mary and Cliffe riding on their bikes and at 11 p.m. when he finished his shift at the chip shop, Absalom called to see her. She was

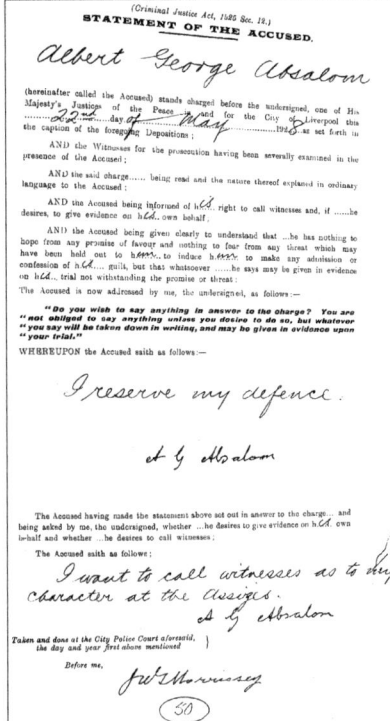

Above left: Mary Alice Read. (*T.J. Leech Archive*)

Above right: Absalom's statement taken following his arrest. (*Author's collection*)

Right: Newspaper cutting relating to the execution of Albert Absalom. (*T.J. Leech Archive*)

ABSALOM
HANGED.

SCENES OUTSIDE WALTON PRISON GATES.

WOMEN'S PRAYERS.

SWEETHEART STABBED TO DEATH.

Albert George Absalom, aged 28, labourer, of Scotland-road, Liverpool, was executed at Walton Prison, Liverpool, at 8 a.m. today for the murder of Mary Alice Reed, aged 26, mill worker, of Garibaldi-street.

A crowd of nearly 200 people, mostly women of the working-class, assembled in Hornby-road opposite the main entrance gates of Walton Prison before the hour of execution, despite a steady drizzle of rain and grey sky.

Most of the onlookers lined the pavement, talking in undertones or gazing silently at the closed gates, while one man passed along distributing tracts.

asleep when he called but woke, dressed and went down to speak to him, assuring him that nothing untoward had occurred. Absalom was not convinced and in a rage he kicked the bike, badly buckling the front wheel.

On the afternoon of 11 May he bought a sheath knife, and about two hours later, he was seen outside St Peter's Church, Sackville Street quarrelling with Mary. Suddenly Mary let out a scream and fell to the ground, clutching her throat. Absalom threw down the knife and ran off down the street but was detained and soon taken into police custody. Asked why he had stabbed the girl, Absalom replied: 'They drive you mad. She won't fool me anymore. I want to be finished with her, she has been playing this game for too long.'

Mary Reed had been stabbed once in the throat and when rushed to hospital, she made a statement claiming that Absalom had stabbed her after she had refused to go out with him that night. She was operated upon that night, but died from her injuries six days later.

Absalom's defence told an incredible story when he appeared before Mr Justice Talbot a month later. Absalom claimed that he had not intended to harm Mary, only to scare her. He said that he had told her he intended to commit suicide and pulled out the knife. Mary had then made to move away from him and he reached out to grab her, forgetting he had the knife in his hand, and she was injured accidentally.

The jury offered a strong recommendation to mercy on the ground that the prisoner was not of a criminal character, and they had been partly swayed by the defence's claim that death had not been directly from the wounds but from causes incidental to her treatment in hospital.

37

HYPNOTIC CHARMS

Joseph Reginald Victor Clarke, 12 March 1929

While taking shelter from a burst of summer rain, smooth-talking Reg Kennedy made the acquaintance of pretty 19-year-old typist, Mary Agnes Fontaine. By the time the shower had subsided, he had persuaded her to go for a drink with him and later that day, she invited him to her home.

'Reg Kennedy' was an alias of 21-year-old Joseph Reginald Victor Clarke. Clarke had been raised by relatives in King's Lynn, Norfolk; his parents had split up before he was born and his mother had returned to her home in Virginia, USA. He was a brilliant scholar, particularly at mathematics, but his schooling was disrupted when his guardian died suddenly. Clarke was sent to America to stay with his mother where he spent a year a Princeton University, before studying with a professor who taught him psychology and hypnotism. It was these hypnotic powers that he used to great effect.

Clarke became a serial seducer, bedding a string of women across the United States, before ending up in Nova Scotia, Canada, where he persuaded one gullible woman to loan him a large sum of money before he fled the country by working his passage to England as a wireless operator on the Transatlantic liner, *Baltic*. Arriving in Southampton, he began to work his

Above left: Hypnotic killer 'Reg Kennedy'. (*Author's collection*)

Above right: Mary Fontaine. (*T.J. Leech Archive*)

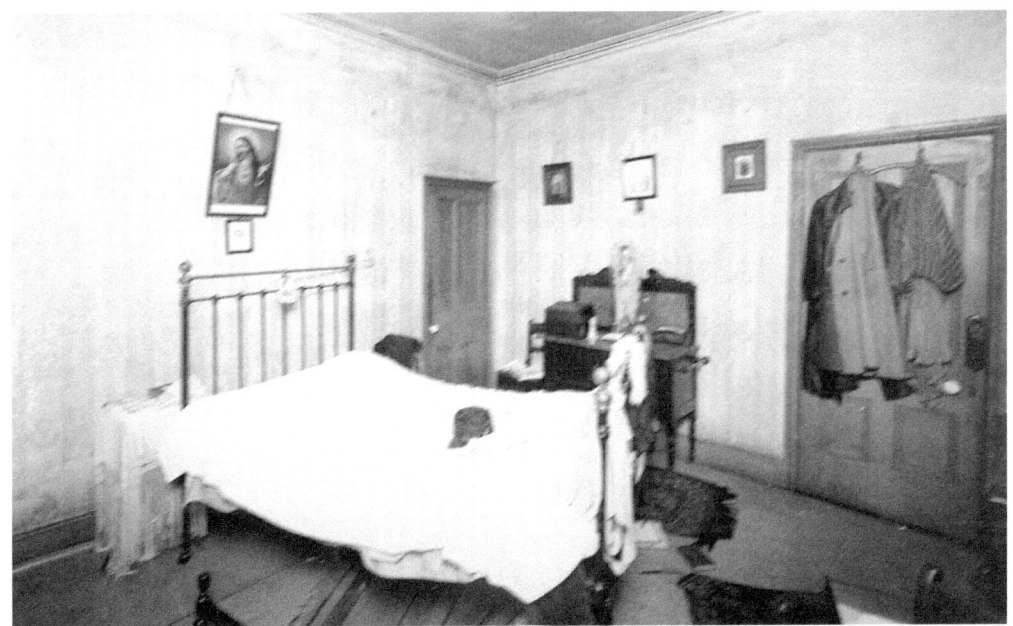

Mary's bedroom where Clarke stabbed and tried to strangle her. (*Author's collection*)

hypnotic charms on a number of women, promising them marriage as they lavished money on him. He moved to the north of England, writing to all of his conquests, keeping them sweet with promises that he would see them soon.

At one point in the summer of 1928 he was courting four sisters from one family in Birkenhead, with each unaware he was bedding the others. When he was finally rumbled, he attempted to strangle the youngest girl with a pyjama cord, but fearing the scandal if the police became involved, the family chose not to report the matter. Later that day, Clarke crossed the Mersey for a fatal rendezvous with Mary Fontaine.

Mary lived with her 47-year-old mother Alice at 110 Northbrook Street, Liverpool, and Clarke's undoubted talent with the female sex was enough for him to persuade them to let him lodge at the house. He was soon carrying on a relationship with both women and persuaded Alice to lend him large sums of money, and to allow him the use of a cellar at the house where he set up a workshop, building, repairing and selling wireless sets.

Despite his obvious intelligence and skill with a wireless, he was not able to make the business a success, and Alice was soon pressing him to repay the money he owed and also to pay his way at the house.

On the morning of Sunday 28 October 1928, Clarke was in the sitting room with Alice Fontaine when she began nagging him again about paying back the money he owed. He suddenly jumped to his feet, put his hands around her throat and squeezed tightly.

When he saw that he had killed her, Clarke then calmly walked into Mary's room and asked her if she loved him. 'I'll always love you, you know I will,' she told him. 'I've just killed mother and I am going to kill you' he told her and attempted to strangle her with a piece of electric flex. Mary fought hard for her life and although he managed to secure the flex around her neck, he suddenly stopped and cut the flex with a knife, as if he had decided no longer to kill her. Mary began screaming and unable to calm her down, Clarke tried to cut her throat but, blood gushing from her neck wound, she was able to push him to the floor and managed to run out into the street where her screams soon had people running to her assistance.

When Clarke appeared at Liverpool Assizes on 4 February 1929, he insisted on pleading guilty to the charges against him. Mr Justice Finlay, having first made sure Clarke understood the implications of such a plea, then proceeded to pass sentence of death. The whole proceedings had lasted less than five minutes.

Following conviction, Clarke was visited every day by Mary Fontaine and he spent the whole time in the condemned cell writing letters, mostly to her, but also to the string of women he had seduced and deceived both in England and North America. He told his counsel that he had bedded over a hundred women in the last three years. A few days before he was to hang he sought permission from the Home Secretary to marry Mary. Despite the horrors of what had happened at her home, it seems Clarke's hypnotic charms were still strong and she accepted his proposal, only for the request to be refused.

Clarke had been in the exercise yard when he observed the workmen constructing the new execution chamber. He turned to one of the other prisoners and told them: 'I suppose I will be the first to experiment with this toy!' As it turned out, the new gallows would not be ready in time and he was hanged on the original gallows in the old coach house.

On the morning of his execution, the Liverpool Echo wrote that a cold, grey, dense fog hung like a pall over the gaol as a crowd of over 200 gathered outside the prison gates to wait for the notices of execution to be posted. It was not recorded if any of his conquests were included in that number. Clarke walked firmly to the gallows, while at that same moment, across the city at St Bernard's Church, Mary Fontaine attended mass, praying and mourning the man who, in a matter of months, had turned her life upside down.

38

'POOR JOHNNY'

John Maguire, 26 November 1929

'I will be hung for you one day,' Johnny Maguire told his wife on more than one occasion. In early 1929 he made the threat again and this time his boasts would be telling.

Forty-three -year-old Maguire worked as a hawker and lived with his wife, Ellen, the mother of his ten children. The eldest of their children was 24 years old and like the other three older children, no longer lived at home. The youngest child was just 18 months and with seven other children at home, the house on Newsham Street, off Scotland Road, was cramped, and a constant hive of activity.

At the time, Ellen Maguire was also six months pregnant, and it seems that her husband had a very jealous nature and was even convinced that another man had fathered one of her young children.

On the afternoon of 5 September, Maguire was out working and when he returned in the afternoon, he began to quarrel with his wife. Earlier, Maguire had called into a pawnbroker's and had purchased a knife and a razor.

Later that afternoon, he called at their neighbour's house and shouted for them to: 'come and see what I have done.' James Kennedy and his wife, Julia accompanied Maguire back to his house where he led them to Ellen, lying dead in the bedroom. As they tried to take in the horror of what they had found, Maguire simply picked up his hat and walked out the door.

The police had already been alerted and a hunt was on for the killer when Maguire finally surrendered that evening, entering a police station and saying he had come to give himself up. He claimed that he had done it in a jealous rage because his wife had been unfaithful.

Ellen Maguire had been stabbed in the back and while she was unconscious on the floor, he had cut her throat several times with the razor. Both weapons used were the ones he had purchased earlier that day.

His trial, before Mr Justice Humphreys on 8 November was a formality. Premeditation was proved by the fact that Maguire had purchased the murder weapons shortly before he had carried out the attack and that he had told several people that he had killed her because she had been unfaithful, thus supplying a motive. A defence of insanity failed to sway the jury and the trial ended with the only possible verdict.

His sister Mary Hagan launched a petition on his behalf and wrote to the Home Secretary, supporting the defence's plea of insanity by claiming that when her brother was a young boy, he had fallen off a wall and badly injured his head. Since then he had suffered fits. She also claimed that several members of their family had been certified insane in the past and injuries Maguire had suffered during his army service in the war had also affected him. It was to no avail.

Maguire was the first person to be executed in the new execution suite. It had been constructed in line with many other prisons around the country and at Walton it was built onto the side of I wing, with an adjacent cell to reduce the length of the walk between the condemned cell and the gallows, and to lessen the time of an execution, which was not taking an average of twenty seconds from the hangman entering the cell to the prisoner being dead at the end of the rope.

Left: Poor Johnny Maguire. (*T.J. Leech Archive*)

Below: Walton Gaol, where crowds gathered to await the signal that Maguire had been executed. (*Liverpool County Record Office*)

On the morning of the execution, Mary Hagan was one of several members of the family waiting outside the gates as the hour drew near. She began wailing and crying that she hadn't said goodbye properly to poor Johnny, but the authorities refused her entry. When she began to bang on the gate hysterically, she was ushered away by officers. As the prisoner bell chimed, signifying that the execution had taken place, she again rushed the gates crying, 'Poor Johnny, oh my poor, poor Johnny!'

39

'A TISSUE OF LIES'

Richard Hetherington, 20 June 1933

The dispute was over money. Thirty-six-year-old farmer Richard Hetherington, of Great Strickland, Westmorland, had done some work for 76-year-old Joseph Nixon, and his wife, Mary Ann, 75, who lived on a farm three miles away at Newby. The dispute was long-running and it seems that Nixon believed that Hetherington owed him money for the rent of some land, and therefore, as they were now straight, Hetherington was refusing to give him a penny more.

Throughout 1932, the feud had simmered and by 1933, matters were coming to a head. On one occasion, police were called to deal with a disturbance at the house. On 17 February, Hetherington purchased a shotgun from a Penrith gunsmith and told a neighbouring farmer that he was having problems with Joseph Nixon and said that he would get even with 'the old twister,' and would sort matters out once and for all.

Early on the morning of Monday 20 February, a neighbouring farmer could smell burning and, going out into his field, he saw smoke bellowing from the Nixons' farmhouse. By the time the firemen and police were at the scene, the house was destroyed with only the brick chimney-stack standing amongst the scorched remnants of the house. The charred remains of Mr and Mrs Nixon were also discovered and when examined, both were found to have died as a result of gunshot wounds – Mrs Nixon had over 200 shotgun pellets in her heart.

It didn't take detectives long to trace Hetherington as the likely suspect and he was quickly placed under arrest. He was adamant that he did not have a gun, but this was soon disproved when the Penrith gun shop owner identified him as the man who had purchased a shotgun prior to the murder. A search of his house later discovered the gun concealed in a barn. When he was searched, he was found to be carrying a wallet, later proved to have belonged to the murdered man.

On 3 May, while on remand at Liverpool, Hetherington made a failed attempt to hang himself with his braces. He was prevented by officers and placed under extra surveillance until he came to trial. When he appeared before Mr Justice MacNaughton at Westmorland Assizes on 29 May, the prosecution put forward a strong case for wilful murder. They had the motive of the money Nixon believed the prisoner had owed him, and the subsequent arguments this had led to. They also had the positive identification of the prisoner having purchased a gun prior to the shooting.

Hetherington's defence was that he had discovered the wallet lying in a field and had intended to hand it in to the police. When his alibi was destroyed – 'a tissue of lies' – the prosecution claimed, his counsel then tried to show that Hetherington was insane. They said that the prisoner had been badly wounded in the war which had led him to behaving irrationally. After a three day trial, the jury took just over three hours to find him guilty and he was sentenced to death. There was no formal appeal and no recommendation to mercy.

Joseph and Mary Nixon. (*Author's collection*)

The remains of the burned out farmhouse. (*Author's collection*)

RICHARD HETHERINGTON FOUND GUILTY.

SENTENCED TO DEATH.

THREE DAYS' TRIAL AT APPLEBY ASSIZES.

Defence's Strong Fight Against Circumstantial Evidence.

RICHARD HETHERINGTON, 36, farmer, Great Strickland, was found guilty at Appleby Assizes on Wednesday of the murder of Joseph Nixon and his wife, Mary Ann Nixon, at their bungalow at East View, Newby, and sentence of death was passed.

The trial lasted three days and the jury were absent three hours and five minutes in considering their verdict.

Mr. Justice MacNaghten, the Judge, said to the jury

"I think you will find there are two incidents of which, when you have formed your opinion, you will have little difficulty in forming your opinion as to the rest.

Newspaper cutting reporting
Hetherington's sentence of death.
(*Author's collection*)

Richard Hetherington under arrest.
(*Author's collection*)

DECLARATION OF SHERIFF

AND OTHERS.

31 Vict. Cap. 24.

We, the undersigned, hereby declare that

Judgment   of   Death   was   this   Day   executed   on

RICHARD. HETHERINGTON.   in His Majesty's Prison of

LIVERPOOL. .... in our presence.

Dated this _twentieth_ day of _June_ 1933.

~~Raymond~~ Un ~~aur~~ Sheriff of   WESTMORLAND.

Justice of the Peace

for   the City of Liverpool.

Governor of the said Prison.

Chaplain of the said Prison.

No. 280.   6189 472/525 250 4/25 146 F A

Left: Notice of Hetherington's execution which was posted on the prison gates. (_Author's collection_)

Below: Hetherington's written appeal to spare his life. (_Author's collection_)

Sir   I regret a portion of what I am in. but it cannot be helped. Under the present situation I shall pray to God. that on behalf my own people that I wish you cons to consider the effects of the Army my nerves was upset, and didst realise what I was doing. I appeal to you under the circumstances that I will pray to God. that I should be reprieved if under the circumstances of my own life. on behalf of my own people.

I remain
Yours faithfully
R^t Hetherington

40

A SAILOR'S REVENGE

Jan Mohamed, 8 June 1938

In the spring of 1938, Indian sailors Jan Mohamed and Aminul Hag were both serving on a steamer for the Hall Line fleet. Thirty-year-old Mohamed had been working for the company for the last ten years with an exemplary record and for the last seven months, the two men had worked together in the engine room, Mohamed as fireman and Hag as a trimmer.

On 15 March 1938 the relationship between the two men changed abruptly. They had a fierce quarrel, and later, as Mohamed slept on his bunk, 20-year-old Hag smashed an iron bar into his friend's face, knocking out several teeth.

Following this incident, the captain kept the two apart, giving them duties on different parts of the ship, and when it reached Gladstone Dock, Liverpool, Hag was transferred to the SS *Kabinga* while Mohamed was given lodgings on Pitt Street, pending the arrival of a new vessel.

The *Kabinga* stayed in port for several days, manned by just a skeleton crew, one of which was Hag. On 9 April, Mohamed was seen attempting to board the SS *Kabinga*, but was thwarted by the chief steward. Two days later he tried again and this time he was able to gain access. Mohamed secreted himself on board and hid in a passage for over three hours until Hag returned. They began to quarrel, during which time Hag was beaten and stabbed to death with a heavy, metal engineer's file.

Tried before Mr Justice Tucker at Liverpool Assizes just sixteen days later, Mohamed claimed that he had acted in self-defence. He said that he had gone on board the vessel to try to make peace with Hag, only for his former friend to turn on him. He alleged that Hag had come at him and Mohamed had simply picked up the first thing to hand.

The prosecution disputed this, claiming that Mohamed had simply concealed himself onboard, waited until Hag appeared and had deliberately battered him to death. In the end, the case rested on a key point. If the fatal wound had been delivered to the front of the body, then it would support a claim of self defence; if, however, the wounds were to the back of the victim, it would suggest wilful murder. Medical evidence confirmed that the blows had been struck from behind and as a result, Mohamed was found guilty of murder.

Mohamed's translated letter written to his mother, following his arrest. (*Author's collection*)

A rough translation of the letter:-

Mother! To me ... ... and I have done a murder in Europe. Maybe the punishment will be hanging: thus it is known. Maybe the King might pardon. God knows whether there will be pardon. If there be no pardon, then hanging. And, Mother, I have made great efforts to come but I could not come. Mother, pray to God for me, and maybe hanging will be pardoned. Then there would be [_Sal_. Prison?]. If it should be [Imprisonment?] I will write another letter - if not, nothing. Mother, had you not left [deserted?] me, I should not have come to this city and I should have stayed with you. But you left me, and I became [...? _darbar_.]. So in this city today this [...? _sala mola_] has come to me. And give many salaams to my Uncle*, - he made me great from little [? brought me up in childhood ?], and his [... ? _yaan_] is over me

41

THE WOUNDED THUMB

Samuel Morgan, 9 April 1941

It was almost closing time at the local newsagents on Sandy Lane, Waterloo, Liverpool, and James Hagan needed his cigarettes and evening newspaper. It was 6.30 p.m. on Saturday 2 November 1940 and, although the whole of Liverpool was observing a wartime blackout, Hagan had no qualms about asking his 15-year-old daughter, Mary to go on the short errand for him. It was a decision he would rue for the rest of his life.

Mary left her house on Brookside Avenue, Waterloo, and when she failed to return home later that night, a search party combed the local area along the route she would have taken to the shop. On the corner of Sandy Lane was a concrete blockhouse next to the bridge over the adjacent railway line, and when one of the search party shined his torch into the dank, soot-stained building, he discovered the body of Mary Hagan.

Mary had been raped and strangled, but the killer had left a vital clue beside the body. A piece of crêpe bandage, the type issued to soldiers, was found in the murky water which had been shaped as if to cover a thumb wound. A witness told detectives that he had seen a soldier loitering near the bridge shortly before Mary would have passed. Crucially, another witness also saw the same soldier, naming him as Sammy Morgan, a private in the First Battalion of the Irish Guards. When detectives went to his unit, they found Morgan had gone absent without leave.

Two weeks later a policeman in Streatham, south London, investigating an assault on a woman, spotted a soldier acting suspiciously. When asked for identification papers, the man fled, but was soon tracked down and arrested on suspicion of the assault. When his identity was revealed, Morgan was returned to Liverpool for questioning regarding the murder of Mary Hagan.

Morgan had a cut to his thumb and when his belongings were searched, a role of dressing was found that matched the piece found beside the body. This became a more conclusive link to the murder when investigations found that the bandage was a faulty reel with a flaw in the stitching. This meant that the chances of the bandage being from another source were very, very unlikely.

The evidence of the bandage formed the main prosecution evidence when Morgan stood trial for murder on 17 February 1941. Further evidence of soil samples taken from the blockhouse matched samples taken from Morgan's uniform. They also had the statement Morgan had made following his arrest in which he had admitted being in the area at the time of the murder but claimed he did not intend to hurt the child at all.

Morgan denied making the statement and claimed that the police had bullied him and written things down in order to secure a conviction. He claimed that on the night of the murder he had been drinking in the Royal Hotel, Seaforth with his brother and friends, who both backed up his claims.

He was sentenced to death by Mr Justice Stable who later told the appeal court that he had no doubt of the condemned man's guilt.

Mary Hagan. (*T.J. Leech Archive*)

Mary Hagan's Fate in Blockhouse

SAMUEL MORGAN wore battle dress when brought into court at Liverpool Assizes this week to face the charge of having murdered Mary Hagan, who was a 15-year-old convent school girl. Mary, at 6-45 p.m. on November 2 had been sent by her father to make purchases

SAMUEL MORGAN.

at a shop in Sandy-lane, Seaforth. She would have to cross a bridge and pass a military blockhouse, and she arrived at the shop by 6.50, but she found it necessary to call at two other shops, the last of which she left shortly after 7 p.m.

That was the last time she was seen alive by anybody, the prosecution, led by Mr. G. Justin Lynskey, K.C., could call upon.

By 7.30, through the girl's non-return home, her parents made inquiry. Search was begun, and shortly after 11 p.m. Mary was found in the blockhouse.

The prosecution's allegation was that while on her way home the girl had either been enticed, or dragged, into the blockhouse and there violated and strangled.

Blockhouse murderer Samuel Morgan.
(*T.J. Leech Archive*)

42

ON A WEEKEND PASS

David Roger Williams, 25 March 1942

At 6.45 p.m. on Sunday 30 November 1941, a couple making their way home in the darkness along Westgate, a lonely road in Morecambe, heard a low moaning noise from across the road. Shining a torch, they found a very distressed woman leaning against a concrete post at the end of a footpath. The woman had no underwear and just one shoe and stocking on, and was soaking wet and shivering with cold. She gave her name as 28-year-old Elizabeth Smith of Pond Terrace, Carnforth, and with the assistance of two passing airmen, she was taken to Queen Victoria Hospital, where before she collapsed, she told a witness that 'David' had attacked her.

While initially diagnosed as suffering from shock and concussion, she quickly developed bronchial pneumonia, although she seemed at first to be responding well to treatment. Detectives at her bedside questioned Elizabeth's family and her sister, Beatrice, told detectives that Elizabeth had been seeing an airman for several weeks and although she believed that he had wanted them to get engaged, Elizabeth had been reluctant for any such commitment and had recently written to him saying that she was ending their relationship.

'David' was David Roger Williams, a 33-year-old aircraftsman from Brecon in South Wales. He was arrested at his former lodgings in Morecambe and told officers he had met Elizabeth when he had been posted to the area a few months before. He said he had travelled up to Morecambe on a weekend pass from his new base in Essex to try to sort out their relationship and that they had met up earlier that evening and gone for a walk in Happy Mount Park. They had then made their way towards Westgate where she had suffered the terrible accident.

He told detectives that they had patched up their differences and Elizabeth had spoken about getting engaged to him the following March. It was then as they were crossing a wooden bridge that she dropped a bombshell and said that she had changed her mind; she had her eye on another airman and was ending their relationship. Williams then claimed that she had fallen off the bridge and landed face down in the water. He had then jumped in after her but was unable to lift her out at first due to the weight of the woman soaked with water, although he did eventually manage it.

Taken into custody, Williams's story was not believed and he was held on a charge of grievous bodily harm. Two days later Elizabeth suffered a relapse and died. A post-mortem found that she had died as a result of shock, inhalation bronchial pneumonia and tuberculosis of one part of the lung.

Detectives went to the scene of the 'accident' and found that the stream was so shallow that the only way Elizabeth could have inhaled the amount of water that she did was if her face was forcibly held down into the water.

There was no doubt that Williams had been present at the time of her death but the question of his responsibility was debated before Mr Justice Oliver at Liverpool Assizes on 4 February. Believing he was responsible, the jury quickly returned a guilty verdict, although they did add a strong recommendation for mercy.

Elizabeth Smith.
(*T.J. Leech Archive*)

The Home Secretary declined to interfere in the verdict when Williams' counsel offered a plea of insanity based on the prisoner being a sexual pervert who, as a youngster, had been caught by his parents repeatedly having sex with animals on the family farm, to the extent that the family had to sell the farm and move away from the countryside. Despite this, the Secretary recorded that it was a brutal murder with no extenuating circumstances.

43

THE LADIES' MAN

Douglas Edmondson, 24 June 1942

Douglas Edmondson was a ladies' man. To the envy of his many friends, it seemed that he had been blessed with a special gift that would often cause women to fight for his attentions. He in turn knew how to use this power, and as a result, he was rarely seen without some pretty young girl on his arm when out on the town in the seaside resort of Southport.

One girl in particular, Imeldred Maria Osliff, was a frequent companion, and in her eyes, at least, she was his fiancée. She had known Edmondson since school and although he had proposed marriage, once they had consummated their relationship, it seems he did not have the same thoughts about the relationship that she did.

At the outbreak of the Second World War, 25-year-old Edmondson left Southport and a string of girlfriends, and travelled down to Plymouth, becoming a petty officer in the Royal Navy. He initially served as a stoker on a convoy ship before being transferred to the carrier

Ark Royal. In November 1941, he was seriously injured when an Italian U-boat torpedoed the ship off Gibraltar. Although many of his shipmates were killed, he was one of the more fortunate ones, though he did sustain a leg injury that left him with a limp and also suffered a badly damaged left arm. It was while recovering from his injuries at Evesham Hospital in the Midlands, that he first met Delia Chatterton. Like Douglas, she too was already in a serious relationship, and although both were technically engaged, their respective partners where elsewhere and they were instantly attracted to each other. Like many women before her, the young nurse soon fell hopelessly in love with the dashing sailor.

Following his discharge from hospital, they returned to his camp on the south coast and married. For a short time Edmondson and his wife were happy enough, and although he received a small pension from a naval trust and found a job with the Government, he soon found himself short of cash. He was then asked by his landlady for £15 to replace a sofa they had damaged and threatened with eviction, he needed to find money quickly. Unable to raise the cash, Edmondson fell back on his natural talents and chose to use his hold over women to acquire a little more money.

In January 1942, leaving his wife at the naval camp, Edmondson returned to Southport, and immediately sought out 28-year-old Imeldred Osliff, still living with her parents on Moss Lane, Banks, Southport, and now working as a nurse in the isolation ward at New Hall, Birkdale, part of the main Southport Hospital. Edmondson wrote asking for her help in a delicate matter. He had neglected to inform her of his marriage, but word had reached back to her, and although angered and upset, she agreed to meet him. Edmondson was staying with an aunt on Norwood Road, Southport when, after tea on Saturday 7 February, he dressed and went out, saying that he had a date for the evening. On that same day Imeldred had left home in the morning to go on duty and walked with her father to the bus stop, telling him that she wouldn't be home for tea as she was meeting Douglas and they were going to the theatre. A man out walking his dog on Victoria Park found her body early the next morning. Lying by the bushes close to the entrance, her clothing had been torn and she had been strangled. Her small black handbag, purse and identity card were all missing.

The distraught parents told the police about their daughter's assignation on the previous evening with the mysterious Douglas, although somewhat shamefully, they admitted to the detectives that they knew nothing about him. Enquiries soon revealed that Imeldred had last been seen at around 9 p.m. with Douglas Edmondson and a short time later, a man matching his description was seen boarding a Liverpool-bound train. Later that Sunday afternoon, police in Liverpool recovered the bag, which contained Imeldred's identity card. Detectives discovered Edmondson had travelled down to Birmingham where, in the early hours of the morning of Tuesday 10 February, he was arrested.

On Monday 20 April, Edmondson stood trial at Liverpool Assizes before Mr Justice Wrottesley. He pleaded not guilty. The prosecution's case was that he had killed Imeldred after she had refused to give him some money. Evidence showed that Edmondson had written to her asking for help, and she had agreed to his request, and that while they were in Victoria Park, Edmondson had strangled her, stealing her handbag containing money and the letters written by him and addressed to her.

The trial lasted two days, and as it drew to a close, the defence realised their only hope in saving Edmondson from the noose was to prove he was insane. His wife testified that he lived in a fantasy world, had a tendency towards 'sheer romance' and at various times during their short marriage, he had told several remarkable tales, including lies such as his brother having been killed in action.

Under questioning, Edmondson admitted that he had strangled Imeldred, but denied robbery was the motive. He said that he had asked for a loan and she had agreed and suggested meeting in the park. They had quarrelled when she became abusive about his wife and he had lost his temper and grabbed her throat. The fact that he had taken her handbag, thus preventing immediate identification, supported the case that it was a murder for gain and the jury took less than thirty minutes to find him guilty of murder.

Above left: Imeldred Osliff. (*T.J. Leech Archive*)

Above right: Ladies' man Douglas Edmondson. (*T.J. Leech Archive*)

The body of Imeldred Osliff was discovered close to the entrance of Victoria Park. (*Author's collection*)

44

TO SOLVE HIS FINANCIAL PROBLEMS

Ronald Roberts, 10 February 1943

Ronald Roberts needed money. He had several pressing debts, and one in particular, to his works' tontine club, was beginning to cause him embarrassment. The 28-year-old shipyard worker could see no immediate solution to his problems until he suddenly hit on an idea.

Roberts shared an upper-floor flat at 2G Brig Street, Barrow-in-Furness with Mrs Catherine Cartwright Worrall and her 17-year-old son. Mrs Worrall was separated from her husband, and all three at the house occupied separate rooms; mother and son each had a bedroom while Roberts slept on a camp-bed in the sitting room.

Roberts' financial problems increased when he began to need time off from his job because of severely ulcerated legs, which caused him intense pain and needed a lot of medical attention. His frequent absences meant a loss in wages, and he addressed this by borrowing small sums of money from the tontine club, of which he was the treasurer. Matters came to a head when, at the end of September 1942, several members of the club asked to see the annual accounts. On top of this, Roberts was being asked to repay several personal debts and to settle a number of various accounts with local tradesmen. In desperation, he put his plan into action.

He had been living at Brig Street for two years and knew that every Monday afternoon, always between 4.30 and 5 p.m., a woman called at the house collecting the weekly money owed by all three tenants to the Midland Clothing Company, which circulated a mail order catalogue. The collector was 37-year-old Mrs Nellie Pearson, and it was she whom Roberts had decided would solve his financial problems.

On Saturday 26 September, Roberts returned to the flat and announced that he had won on a football coupon. 'I've come up on the pools,' he rejoiced, 'two lines. I've won eight pounds eight shillings.' A few days later, he returned to Brig Street with more than £6, which he claimed had been given to him by a local grocer, who had cashed the winning pools' coupon cheque.

To his fellow tenants, it seemed that Roberts's luck may have changed for the better. Not only had he won modestly on the pools, but he was also allowed to change his labouring job to the less strenuous role of fire watching at the Vickers Armstrong Shipyard.

On the evening of Monday 5 October, Mrs Worrall returned home from work and was unable to gain entry. The same thing had happened on the previous Monday, when Roberts had pretended not to be at home when Mrs Pearson had called to collect the catalogue money. This week it was Mrs Worrall's turn to pay and she had left the money with her card on the mantelpiece with a note asking Roberts to pay Mrs Pearson. Catherine Worrall sat on the stairs chatting to a neighbour for ten minutes until Roberts returned, apologising for locking her out, saying he had been to the pictures and had forgotten the club lady was due.

Roberts seemed agitated but claimed he was in pain from his legs, though she did notice that his run of good fortune was continuing as he was clutching another wad of pound notes, claiming he had collected some back pay from work.

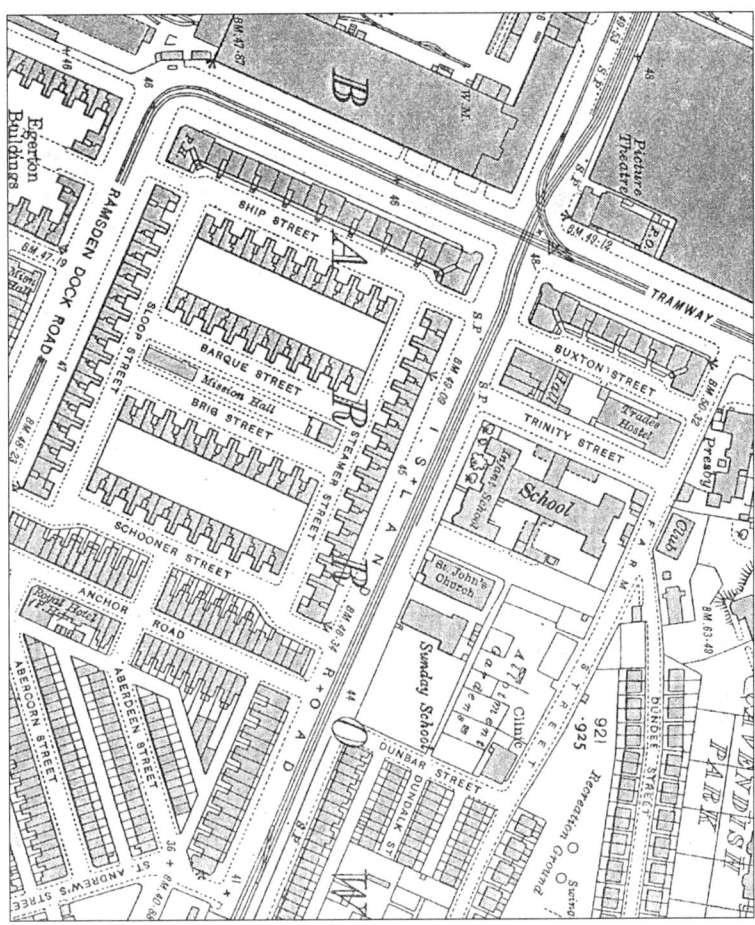

Above: Ordinance Survey Street plan of the Brig Street area of Barrow. (*TNA:PRO*)

Right: Victim Nellie Pearson. (*Author's collection*)

END OF BARROW FLAT CRIME TRIAL

Jury Reject "Guilty But Insane" Plea

SUPPORTED by two warders, Ronald Roberts (28), of 2G, Brig-street, Barrow, made no comment when, after donning the Black Cap, Mr. Justice Stable at Manchester Assizes yesterday evening passed sentence of death after the jury found him guilty of the murder of Mrs. Nellie Pearson (39), a clothing club collector, of Undergreens-road, Barrow, on 5 October.

Throughout the trial, which lasted two and a half days, Roberts had appeared to take little interest in the proceedings. He sat between two warders in the dock tightly clenching a handkerchief with which he occasionally dabbed his eyes.

The case for the prosecution was that Roberts owed money to tradesmen and a works tontine club, of which he had been treasurer, and that he murdered was not in his right mind when the crime was committed.

"Members of the jury, where is that evidence?" he asked There is no history of insanity in his family or a shred of evidence that before or after 5 October, he suffered from any disease of the mind.

The jury, of which three of the 12 members were women, returned their verdict within 15 minutes.

Newspaper cutting relating to Ronald Roberts' conviction. (*Author's collection*)

Hangman Thomas Pierrepoint became the subject of a Home Office enquiry following his execution of Barrow murderer Ronald Roberts. (*Author's collection*)

'Perhaps you can pay off some of your debts,' she suggested, bearing in mind that her sister was one of those to whom Roberts owed money. Roberts promised he would and in the next twenty-four hours, he went on a spending spree, settling all his debts in full and splashing out on several rounds of drinks at the tontine club.

The following night headlines in the local newspaper reported that Mrs Pearson was missing. Detectives searched the area without success and began to track down the customers she had visited on her rounds on the Monday evening. This led police to Brig Street and on Thursday 8 October, detectives questioned Roberts.

All three occupants were there, and when told that they believed Mrs Pearson had been there on Monday evening, Roberts said she may have been but he hadn't seen her as he had been at the cinema. He handed officers the unstamped club card to support his claims. Detectives told Roberts they had witnesses who had seen him on Brig Street at around 4.30 p.m. when Nellie Pearson would have called at the house. Roberts then claimed that he had left the pictures early but still denied having seen Mrs Pearson.

Officers weren't satisfied with Roberts' account of his movements and asked to search the house. They entered the bedroom of Mrs Worrall where they discovered the body of Nellie Pearson concealed in an alcove in the bedroom, hidden behind some furniture. Unbeknown to her, Catherine Worrall had been sleeping within feet of the dead body for the last four nights!

Roberts was tried at Manchester Assizes before Mr Justice Stable on 11 December. The prosecution's case was based around an admission Roberts had made after his arrest. They stated that it was a brutal murder for gain and that after being battered about the head with a blunt instrument, the victim had been stabbed to death in the throat. The two attacks had been several hours apart, which suggested that Roberts must have carried out the second attack while Mrs Worrall was home from work, most likely when she had popped outside to speak to a neighbour.

There was also evidence that Roberts had sexually assaulted the stricken woman and his counsel, to further their claim that Roberts was insane, used this as the basis for their defence. They also claimed that the pain Roberts was suffering from his ulcerated legs caused him severe depression to the extent that he was unaware of his actions at the time of the murder. The jury took less than fifteen minutes to find Ronald Roberts guilty and on a cold February morning two months later, Nellie Pearson was avenged.

45

THE WOMAN IN THE CELLAR

Thomas James, 29 December 1943

Good-time girl Gwendoline Sweeney preferred to spend her time in the bars and cafés around the docks, supplementing her income by working as a prostitute, with her clients being mainly West Indian sailors. On Tuesday 17 August 1943, she spent the evening drinking heavily with one of her 'boyfriends', 26-year-old Thomas James, a half-caste marine fireman, known to his friends as Knocker.

Left: Thomas James. (*Author's collection*)

Below: Entrance to 4 Kitchen Street. (*Author's collection*)

Kitchen Street was bombed several times during the early years of the Second World War.
(*Author's collection*)

By 8.30 p.m., they were in the Bush Hotel St James Street, where they were joined by a friend of James', George Dias. All three were drinking heavily and upon leaving the pub, James and Gwendoline went into an air-raid shelter while Dias waited outside. A few minutes later a policeman entered the shelter and ordered them out. The officer watched them walk along Duke Street where Dias joined them.

James and Gwendoline reached a bombed-out house on Kitchen Lane and he told his friend that he wanted to be left alone and would meet up with him later. Dias didn't see his friend again until the following morning when James called to see him and said he was worried about 'Gwennie'. The two men went back to Kitchen Lane where they discovered her body lying in the rubble. They parted and when Dias returned home, he discussed with his wife what had happened.

She advised him to go to the police and later that day, police officers entered the bombed-out house and discovered the mutilated body of Gwendoline Sweeney lying in a pool of blood in the cellar. She was naked and had been sexually assaulted a number of times with a broken bottle and a yard brush, but the cause of death was strangulation.

James lodged at a house at 65 Upper Warwick Street, and was arrested there that evening. He had a long criminal record and had served time in borstal and in prison for a variety of violent assaults and larceny. He denied any involvement in the murder of Gwendoline Sweeney but made a fatal slip-up when questioned by detectives.

James said that if he was going to commit murder, he wouldn't strangle them, he would knife them. No mention had been made of the cause of death and it was enough for him to be charged with wilful murder.

When the case came to trial at Liverpool Assizes on 5 November, his counsel put forward a defence that the cause of death was accidental and that James had been too drunk on the night to realise what he had been doing and that he should instead be found guilty of manslaughter. They claimed that the victim was a sexual pervert in the sense that she allowed her clients to have both natural and un-natural intercourse with her. On the night of her death, Gwendoline had, during sexual intercourse, allowed James to insert a broom handle inside her and during sex, she had fallen and the broom handle had caused her fatal internal injuries.

Medical experts easily disproved this. They claimed that the broom and broken glass had been used on the victim after she had been strangled.

Following arrest, James had caused great concern to the prison staff while in custody, telling guards that he knew he was 'going down' and that he would kill someone in the prison before he did. Returned to Walton for execution, extra guards were placed on stand-by, should James try to carry out his threat. As it turned out, the execution was carried out so quickly that the prisoner did not have time to struggle before he was pinioned and on the scaffold.

46

A LIFE FOR A LIFE

John Gordon Davidson, 12 July 1944

'It says in the bible a life for a life . . . our son has been away fighting in Italy since the outbreak of the war and wants to know if this is what he is fighting for. All we desire is that the death sentence is carried out and he is hung . . . if he gets imprisonment he will still have a life . . . my husband and I will never be the same again.'
(Letter written by Mr and Mrs Appleton to the Home Secretary, June 1944)

On the evening of Sunday 19 April 1944, two young soldiers in the R.A.O.C. stationed at Rainford, west Lancashire, decided to have a night on the town. Leaving their barracks, the two men, John Sanderson and 18-year-old Scots born John Davidson, went into St Helens and spent the early part of the evening drinking in the Rifle Corps Hotel, where they chatted with other soldiers and a number of girls.

Around 10 p.m., Sanderson and Davidson, having paired off, left in the company of two girls and went to get more drink. The girl Davidson had his eye on had only come out to accompany her friend and now that her friend had gone off with her man, she had no interest in the young Scotsman, and she quickly bid Davidson goodnight and left him on his own.

Davidson went back in search of drink and at closing time, he made his way home when he accosted a woman, Jeannie Galvin, also making her way home and tried to impose himself on her. Fortunately, they were already at her front gate when he tried to kiss her and she pushed him away and darted up the path, with the drunken soldier trampling on her lawn as he tried to catch up with her.

Twenty-seven-year-old Gladys May Appleton had spent the evening visiting her boyfriend, George Baker, in St Helens and as she was working in the morning, she left around 10.40 p.m. Barker had offered to walk her home but as it was only a short distance, she told him that she would be fine and after they kissed goodnight, he watched her walk down the lane and out of sight.

On the following morning, the post woman delivering mail to the headquarters of the National Fire Service at The Elms, on Cowley Hill Lane, discovered Gladys' body lying on the lawn. Her killer had dragged Gladys into a front garden and strangled her with her scarf, forcing a considerable length of it into her mouth, before tearing off her clothes and attempting to rape her. There were also teeth marks on one of her breasts.

Several witnesses had seen the drunken Scottish soldier in the vicinity of Cowley Hill Lane, and the young lady he had tried to force himself on told police of her near escape. Detectives went to her house on Gamble Avenue where they found a clear set of footprints in the soil beside the path.

Their investigations led detectives to the camp at Rainford where Davidson was in custody, having been charged with being absent without leave for a time following the murder. He initially denied the crime but later broke down and made a detailed statement admitting the offence.

Above left: Gladys Appleton. (*Author's collection*)

Above right: The Elms, St Helens. (*Author's collection*)

Below: The body of Gladys Appleton lying on the lawn at The Elms. (*TNA: PRO*)

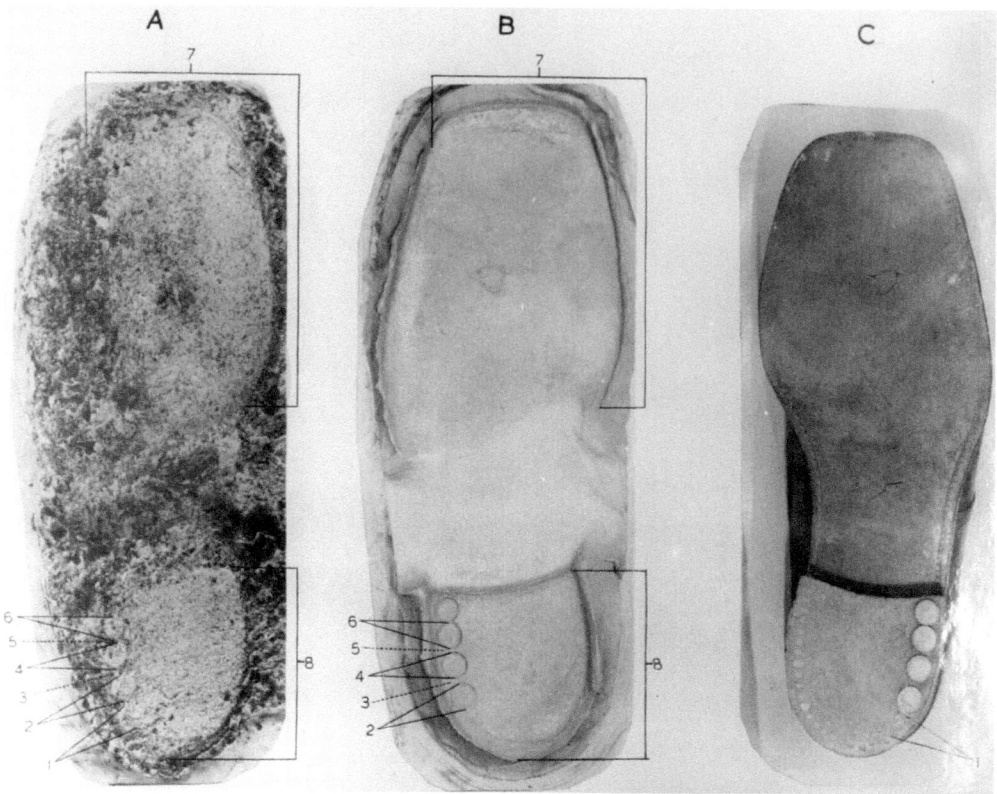

Davidson's tell-tale footprints. (*Author's collection*)

At his trial before Mr Justice Hilbery at Manchester Assizes on 8 May, Davidson's defence was insanity as the prisoner had been so drunk at the time of the crime that he was unaware of his actions. His counsel said that Private Davidson was an illegitimate child who had been brought up by a foster mother. Since leaving school at the age of 14, he had held various casual posts, including some as barman in public houses, before being conscripted.

There was no proof that Davidson was insane and his counsel was unable to call any medical evidence to support their claims. They had suggested to Dr James Murdoch, Medical Officer at Manchester Prison, that the violence used by the prisoner in his attack on the woman might indicate a state of post-epileptic automatism at the time, but while Murdoch agreed that it might, he would not agree that the prisoner was otherwise legally insane.

The jury returned a verdict of murder and added a strong recommendation to mercy. The judge remarked that no other verdict was possible. An appeal was launched but the Court of Criminal Appeal dismissed it with the observation that it was quite clear that Davidson was not insane. It was noted on his file that it was a brutal and sadistic crime, and there were no extenuating circumstances except the prisoner's bad home surroundings and his lack of any parental care and his illegitimacy, which were said to have weighed on his mind and induced a brutal attitude in him towards women who teased or resisted him.

In debating whether to suggest a reprieve, they considered the prisoner's youth. This had moved the trial jury to offer a very strong recommendation to mercy. Home Secretary Herbert

Above left: A petition calling for a reprieve of John Davidson failed to sway the Home Secretary. (*Author's collection*)

Above right: Notice of the execution of John Davidson. (*Author's collection*)

Morrison referred to the case of Leslie Hammond who had committed the brutal murder of a cinema manager in Dover. Hammond was reprieved because he had been just 18 when he had carried out the attack. The Home Office had made it an unwritten rule that the practice should be to reprieve persons under the age of 19 at the time of the commission of the crime, except in the worst cases.

While the issue was being debated, and a campaign was gaining publicity for the reprieve of the young soldier, the victim's parents wrote a short letter to the Home Office, putting forward their point of view in support of his conviction.

Davidson was just three weeks short of his 19th birthday at the time of the murder, and in dismissing the appeal, the Home Secretary recorded his decision by stating: 'This is among the types of cases which I contemplated as exceptional. It is, I think, important that nobody should think even somewhat lightly of this horrible sort of crime – particularly in wartime.'

47

IN THE BASEMENT BROTHEL

Thomas Hendren, 17 July 1946

Detectives in Liverpool suspected that Bobby's Gentleman's Manicurist Saloon on Tempest Hey was being used for immoral purposes and decided to place it under observation. In 1940, they had prepared a file against Gladys Henderson and Ella Valentine Staunton for running similar premises, but before the case could go further, Mrs Henderson was killed in an air raid and the investigation was closed.

On the afternoon of Monday 20 May 1946, two plain-clothed detectives were watching the premises through a spy-hole in the upstairs building when they saw Ella Staunton, the 41-year-old owner, offer a drink to a customer. After a few minutes, the man left the booth and the detectives heard sounds of a struggle. By the time the officers had made their way to the front door, a man was leaving. Asked for some identification, the man offered his National ID card bearing the name Thomas Hendren with an address in Birkenhead. As one of the detectives knocked at the door, Hendren told him he was wasting his time.

'There's a man in there, she won't answer for a quarter of an hour or twenty minutes. You know what Ella is, she's a prostitute,' he told them. Hendren said that he was in a hurry to get back to Birkenhead, and was allowed to leave.

After no reply to their constant banging on the door, the officers forced entry and discovered the body of Ella Staunton. She was lying on her back, her head covered in blood, and a piece of lighting flex was tied around her neck. Splashes of blood were visible on the walls and carpets. She had been the victim of a vicious attack and a bloodstained case opener, resembling a small crowbar, was found in the kitchen area. Although it appeared she had been strangled and battered, death was due to a knife wound to the breast.

The hunt for Thomas Hendren, a 31-year-old unemployed ships baker, took three days and led officers to Salford where he was arrested and charged with murder.

Since leaving the Merchant Navy, Hendren had failed to hold down any type of work and spent his time gambling and drinking. He had recently served a short term of imprisonment for attempted suicide. Following his arrest, Hendren confessed: 'All I want to say is that I did it. She's had plenty out of me, over a hundred pounds in the five years I've known her and when I asked her to lend me a couple of quid she wouldn't, so it happened. I got about ten pounds out of her handbag, a five pound note and five ones.'

Hendren stood trial at Liverpool Assizes before Mr Justice Oliver on Thursday 27 June 1946. The Crown's case was simply that Hendren had murdered Ella Staunton. By his own confession Hendren was a frequent visitor at 'Bobby's Saloon', and he had killed Mrs Staunton after she had refused to loan him a sum of money.

Although the evidence against Hendren was conclusive, the case was far from a formality with the defence basing their case on the issue of insanity. His mother told the court that her son had been well-behaved and law abiding until he had left the Merchant Navy in 1945. While serving in Singapore, he had been given the duty of going ashore to help bury some of the dead. Due to the large number of bodies, it had been impossible to bury them all and as a result, they had to be piled into human bonfires as petrol was poured onto them and they were

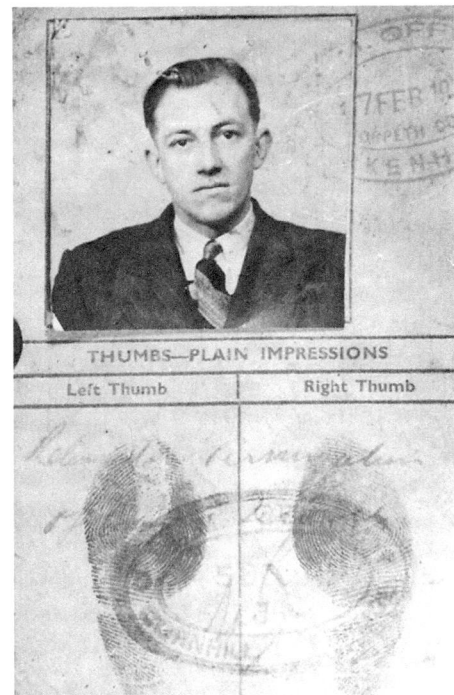

Above left: The doorway leading to Bobby's Saloon. (*Author's collection*)

Above right: Thomas Hendren's ID Card. (*Author's collection*)

Right: The body of Ella Staunton, murdered in the basement brothel. (*TNA: PRO*)

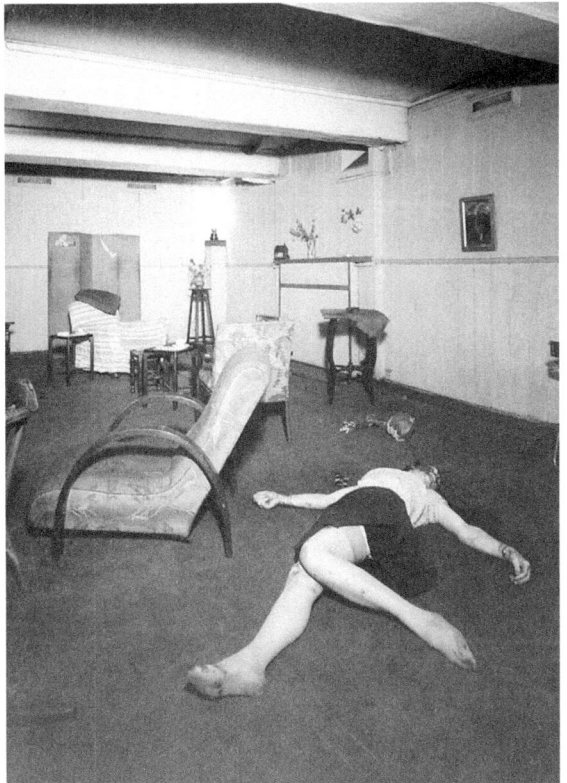

MANICURIST MURDERED IN HER SALOON

Stabbed, flex round her neck

Express Staff Reporter: Liverpool, Tuesday morning

C.I.D. officers last night found Mrs Ella Staunton, 30-year-old, tall, honey blonde manicurist, stabbed through the heart, on the head, and in the face, and with a flex torn from an electric table lamp round her neck, in her saloon at Tempest Hey, in the city centre here.

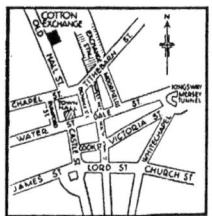

THE SALOON where Ella Staunton was found stabbed and strangled is in Tempest Hey, connecting Dale-street and Tithebarn-street.

Police said: "We want to interview a man in connection with the murder."

They believe some of the girl's wounds were made with a sharp knife, and others by an instrument for taking out nails from wooden boxes which they found in the saloon.

Heard scream

Ella Staunton, who was also known by her maiden name of Ella French, was found shortly after five o'clock by two C.I.D. men who were on plain clothes duty a few yards from her saloon in Tempest Hey, a narrow alley between tall warehouses and business offices leading from Dale-street to Exchange Station.

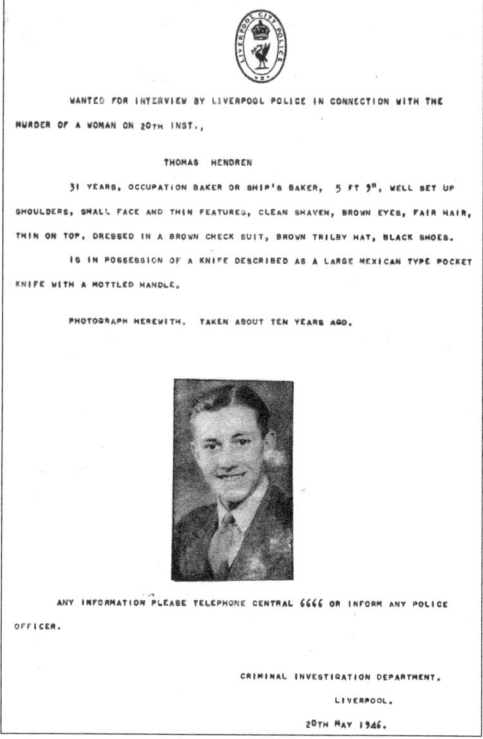

WANTED FOR INTERVIEW BY LIVERPOOL POLICE IN CONNECTION WITH THE MURDER OF A WOMAN ON 20TH INST.,

THOMAS HENDREN

31 YEARS, OCCUPATION BAKER OR SHIP'S BAKER, 5 FT 9", WELL SET UP SHOULDERS, SMALL FACE AND THIN FEATURES, CLEAN SHAVEN, BROWN EYES, FAIR HAIR, THIN ON TOP, DRESSED IN A BROWN CHECK SUIT, BROWN TRILBY HAT, BLACK SHOES.

IS IN POSSESSION OF A KNIFE DESCRIBED AS A LARGE MEXICAN TYPE POCKET KNIFE WITH A MOTTLED HANDLE.

PHOTOGRAPH HEREWITH. TAKEN ABOUT TEN YEARS AGO.

ANY INFORMATION PLEASE TELEPHONE CENTRAL 6666 OR INFORM ANY POLICE OFFICER.

CRIMINAL INVESTIGATION DEPARTMENT.

LIVERPOOL.

20TH MAY 1946.

Above left: Newspaper cutting relating to the murder of Ella Staunton. (*Author's collection*)

Above right: Wanted poster in the Hendren case. (*Author's collection*)

set alight. All aspects of his insanity stemmed from this period. Returning home that year, he had tried to gas himself and had taken 120 tablets in an unsuccessful attempt at suicide, which had resulted in a prison sentence.

Summing up the evidence, the judge asked the jury to consider if they believed that Hendren, when he entered the basement brothel, knew what he was doing, and that if he did, did he know that what he was doing was wrong. After a short consideration, they returned to find him guilty as charged.

48

FIVE-DAY LOVE AFFAIR

Walter Clayton, 7 August 1946

It was a young girl making her way home from the cinema on the night of Friday 12 April 1946 who discovered the body. Alighting from the bus at the Beach Street stop, Bare, the girl walked across the deserted promenade to the sea wall and spotted the body of a young woman lying on the beach.

The police were called and found that the woman had been strangled by the scarf knotted tightly around her neck. There appeared to be no sign of sexual interference; her clothing wasn't dishevelled, which suggested to detectives that she hadn't been dragged to a spot. Within the hour, a wireless car and bloodhounds were at the scene and a generator was set up as police searched for clues under powerful arc lights.

From papers found in the girl's handbag, police discovered she was 23-year-old Joyce Jacques, who had lived on Christie Avenue, Morecambe. Investigations at the house revealed that she was a native of Barnsley who had moved to Morecambe when her parents split up. In 1941 she had enlisted in the WAAF, rising to the rank of Flight Sergeant before her discharge, when she began training as a nurse but quit suddenly and found work in a laundry.

Police also learned that she was something of a 'good-time girl' and that during the last week, Joyce had had an intense relationship with a soldier named Pat, and they had spent every night together since they met.

From papers found in her bedroom, police learned that Pat was one Walter Clayton. Twenty-two-year-old Clayton was a married man recently demobbed, who was in Morecambe staying with his wife's parents on nearby Balmoral Road. Detectives called at the house in the early hours of Saturday and spoke to Clayton. He was reluctant to talk in front of his wife and family and asked to be taken to the police station where he made a full confession.

He told officers he was a native of Clitheroe, Lancashire, where he had married his wife soon after the war broke out. With Clayton overseas, his wife moved back to her parents in Morecambe and on his discharge, Clayton returned to Morecambe, staying with his wife's family while they sorted out a place of their own.

On 5 April he met Joyce Jacques in a ballroom, and they began an intense affair. On 10 April, he had arranged to meet Joyce and she told him she was ending their relationship. They began to quarrel but made up quickly and went out drinking in several pubs.

They ended the night at the Elms public house and Clayton said that Joyce had been drunk and wanted some fresh air. They had walked along the front and he then strangled her with her scarf. Leaving her on the beach, he took a taxi back into town and then went to the Central Pier, where he confessed what he had done to his wife. They had then made their way home and had not long arrived when the police called.

On Wednesday 16 July Clayton stood trial at Manchester Assizes. Wearing his khaki uniform and sporting his service medals and chevrons, he glanced around the court, rubbing his nose nervously as the charge was read out. He replied that he was guilty. To satisfy himself that the prisoner was aware of the consequences, Mr Justice Stable leaned forward and asked him a number of questions:

Confessed to Morecambe Murder

SENTENCED TO DEATH IN TWO MINUTES

Within two minutes of stepping into the dock at Manchester Assizes to-day, Walter Clayton (22), 63, Balmoral-road, Morecambe and Heysham, had been sentenced to death by Mr Justice Stable for the murder at the resort on April 12 of Joyce Jaques (22), who had been staying in lodgings in Christie-avenue.

The Judge put three questions to make sure that Clayton, after he had pleaded guilty, fully understood what he had pleaded and what the consequences would be. The Judge's last question was: " You appreciate that to plead guilty to a charge of

after his arrest Clayton said he first met her in an hotel on April 5. They went by taxi to her home, and he had stayed overnight there and returned to 63, Balmoral-road each morning for the following six days.

Referring to the night of the girl's death, the statement continued: " Joyce said she felt a little drunk, so we decided to go for a stroll along the sea front, where we had a quarrel and I strangled her with my silk scarf. I then left her on the beach."

The statement added that afterwards Clayton met his wife on Central Pier, described what had happened, and told her he had fallen in love with Joyce. " She asked me to go home with

Sobbing Wife

The only sound in court was the sobbing of Clayton's wife, who in a seat behind the dock was the nearest person to her husband apart from the warders beside him and the members of the bar just in front. The Judge gave her permission to meet her husband.

Speaking to the jury after Clayton had left the court the Judge said he wished to point out that the man had had the advantage of being legally represented and that the consequences of a plea of guilty had been fully explained by his counsel. Further he had been under close medical scrutiny and the evidence was that he was in full possession of his senses and perfectly capable of forming a judgment and coming to a decision on so grave a

Above: Police comb the beach at Morecambe. (Morecambe Visitor)

Left: Clayton was sentenced to death in a trial lasting just two minutes. (*Author's collection*)

Judge: Clayton, do you fully understand the nature of the charge to which you have pleaded guilty?

Clayton: [loudly] Yes, my Lord.

Judge: You appreciate what pleading guilty to this charge – that you took this woman's life, with no mitigating circumstances involves?

Clayton: Yes, my Lord.

The commissioner of the Assizes asked him if he had anything to say as to why sentence of death should not be passed, Clayton replied in a firm voice: 'No, my Lord.'

Clayton's eyes were then fixed to the floor as the judge pronounced sentence. The whole proceedings had taken less than three minutes, and as Clayton was ushered from the dock, his wife could be heard sobbing loudly at the back of the court. There was no appeal, but the defence counsel petitioned that the sentence be commuted on the grounds of insanity. The petition was rejected and Clayton, who had committed a brutal murder at the end of an intense five-day love affair, paid for his crime.

Among the victim's possessions, detectives had found a diary which contained an entry written by Joyce with the fatal prophecy: 'I know that one day you'll murder me because your passion gets the better of you.'

49

'MY LOST LOVE'

Arthur Rushton, 19 November 1946

Arthur Rushton no longer saw himself as a married man. Although he had a wife of some six years, to him the marriage had ended in 1945 when he returned from serving overseas and discovered that his wife had been carrying on with other men.

Rushton, a native of Birkenhead, had joined the armed forces in 1938, at the age of 23, and while on leave in Bootle, he met his wife-to-be, Josephine. In June 1940, with Rushton facing an imminent overseas posting, the couple married at Bootle Registry Office.

Word of his wife's infidelity had already reached Rushton and when he returned to Birkenhead in January 1945, instead of returning to his wife, he went to stay with his parents. In his eyes the marriage was now over. It was she, however, who proceeded to file for a divorce on the grounds of desertion, but when the courts rejected this, Rushton himself began proceedings, only to halt them when he ran out of money to continue.

Early in 1946, Rushton met Catherine 'Rene' Cooper, a pretty 17-year-old who worked in the Co-op laundry at Prenton, Birkenhead. With an attractive, babyish face, Rene was the eldest of seven children, and despite the relatively large age gap between her and Rushton, there was an instant attraction between them. They began to meet up almost every day. For Rushton, this was the romance he had always wanted. He courted Rene attentively and showered her with gifts and affection.

Rushton finally confessed to Rene that he was already married, although the marriage was over and he was waiting for a divorce. In today's society, such things are commonplace and hardly cause a murmur, but over sixty years earlier, there was a certain stigma attached to being divorced, which was often enough to end many a relationship. Rene accepted his story but suggested they keep it from her parents.

On Rene's 18th birthday, 30 June 1946, she and Rushton announced their engagement. Her mother threw a party for the couple and Rushton continued to shower Rene with gifts, one of which was a souvenir German dagger. The wartime souvenir had belonged to his brother but when Rene told him she would like to own a knife like that, he bought the dagger and presented it to her at the party.

Then fate intervened. A few days after the party, Rushton's mother called to see Rene's parents and explained that her son was legally still a married man, and had two young children. She said that although he wanted a divorce, there was nothing being done about it. Rene's parents took the news angrily. They felt deceived by a man whom they had begun to look upon as a prospective son-in-law, and as a result, they told Rene that they no longer gave their blessing to the engagement and wanted her to end it. She told Rushton, she must obey her parents' wishes and although she still loved him dearly, the engagement would have to be called off.

Rushton was devastated. He brooded for days and paid several visits to see Rene. He told her that he was unable to pay the costs for a divorce himself, but he knew of a solution. He said that if he re-enlisted in the army, they had a way of arranging speedy divorces for soldiers with adulterous wives. The only drawback to this was that they would be apart for long periods.

Police photos of Arthur Rushton taken following his arrest for a crime before the outbreak of the war. (*Author's collection*)

Rene was now unsure about their relationship and his repeated visits always seemed to end in a quarrel, which led to a rift between them. Finally, at the end of August, he accepted that the engagement was over; told Rene he was going to rejoin his old unit and asked her to return some of the gifts he had given her.

On Monday 2 September, Rushton called at Rene's parents' house on Price Street, Birkenhead, and asked her if he could have a word with her. A few minutes later, Rene came out of the house carrying a buff envelope and the German dagger, which she handed back to him as they walked behind the Birkenhead North End Library. In tears, Rushton asked her if she still loved him. 'Yes, I always will do', she said, herself bursting into tears. Rushton told her that he was going to join the army to get his divorce and she sobbed loudly, saying she would never leave him.

A young girl watching the scene unfold from her window suddenly saw the man strike out at Rene with his fists. Fourteen-year-old Flora Porter saw the attack and shouted for her mother, who joined her just as Rushton pulled out the dagger and plunged it into Rene's chest. As Rene staggered towards her home, Rushton walked away in the opposite direction and seemed to be struggling to put the knife into his raincoat pocket.

Rene collapsed in the doorway of her home and an ambulance was summoned. As she was being helped into the back, Rushton appeared on Price Street. He watched in horror and began to follow the ambulance as it sped towards the hospital. Although it was only a few minutes away, Rene Cooper was dead on arrival.

Rushton made his way to the hospital where, learning that he had killed the woman he loved, he took out a bottle of disinfectant which he gulped down in an attempt to end his own life. He was found collapsed in the hospital grounds and taken inside for emergency treatment.

DAGGER BLOW "A MYSTERY"

Rushton Tells Court

DIVORCE PLAN

The loss of an ordnance map caused the prosecution some difficulty, to-day, at Chester Assizes, where Arthur Rushton, 31-years-old labourer, of Victoria Road, Higher Tranmere, pleaded not guilty of murdering, on September 2, Catherine (Rene) Cooper, aged 18, of Price Street, Birkenhead.

Mr. H. Glyn Jones, K.C., prosecuting with Mr. G Lind Smith, explained that the plans of the district prepared for the jury were photographs of a pre-war ordnance sheet from which the photographer had eliminated parts of Birkenhead destroyed by enemy action.

WOMAN RESWORN

Rushton was represented by Mr. Matabele Davies, K.C., and Mr. J. Jones Roberts.

One of two women on the jury had to be resworn because she kept her gloves on.

Mr. Glyn Jones said Catherine Cooper and Rushton became engaged on her eighteenth birthday, June 30. although he had a wife.

On August 4 Mrs. Cooper gave a lttle party in her house, and Rushton showed a knife to some children. The murder was committed with this, the prosecution claimed.

Rene Cooper's parents heard he was married from Rushton's mother. He admitted it next time he called.

They left it to their daughter to decide her future conduct towards him, and they met from time to time.

All communications should be addressed to "The Governor" and not to any official by name.

H. M. Prison, Liverpool.

5th.November.1946.

Dear Sir,

<u>6796. Arthur Rushton.</u>

The above named has been received into custody at this prison under sentence of death. The execution has been provisionally fixed for Tuesday,19th.November and the Prison Commissioners have elected you to carry out the duties of Assistant Executioner. I enclose herewith two copies of 'Memorandum of Conditions' for your guidance , one copy for your retention and one copy to be signed and returned to me, in acceptance of this appointment.

Should the prisoner appeal you will be notified immediately.

Yours faithfully,

<u>Governor.</u>

Above left: Newspaper cutting relating to the murder of Rene Cooper. (*Author's collection*)

Above right: Letter engaging the services of the assistant executioner. (*Author's collection*)

Rushton's love poem to Rene. (*Author's collection*)

You will not be far away;
Sometimes, when I rest and pray
I shall know your spirits near.
Sweetheart, God bless you. May his might,
Gird your soul and give me share
In your work, and joy, and prayer,
Till I join you in the light.

A. Rushton

For my lost Love — Rene.

Rushton was given urgent medical attention but when it became clear that his life was in no immediate danger, detectives at his bedside charged him with murder. 'I loved her and wanted to go with her. I wanted to live with her. They would not leave us alone. I wanted to die with her,' Rushton said following his arrest.

Rushton stood trial at Chester Assizes on Thursday 31 October 1946 before Mr Justice Lynskey. The prosecution claimed that Rushton had lost his temper after Rene had returned his gifts and in a rage, he had stabbed and fatally wounded her. He had then discarded the weapon and attempted suicide by swallowing the disinfectant.

Rushton merely claimed that he had no recollection of stabbing Rene, and was distraught when he realised what he had done, whereupon he then he tried to end his own life. While awaiting execution, Rushton penned a number of poems, one of which ended poignantly 'til I join you in the light' which he signed 'for Rene, my lost love'.

Rene Cooper wasn't the first person to meet a violent end on Price Street, Birkenhead: twenty years before, Lock Ah Tam brutally murdered his wife and daughters just a few blocks along the same street.

50

BENEATH THE FLOORBOARDS

Stanley Sheminant, 3 January 1947

'I think I have made one big mistake about this whole affair. I should have gone straight to the police instead of trying to conceal this.'

(Statement by Stanley Sheminant following his arrest)

For eight weeks, the military police had been regular visitors to the neat terrace house on Cromwell Street, Hanley, Staffordshire, and always with the same question: did the occupants know the whereabouts of Private Harry Berrisford? Berrisford had been posted as a deserter from the Catering Corps stationed in Lincolnshire since failing to return to his unit after a short leave at the end of May 1946. Replying to the 'Red Caps', Mrs Berrisford gave the same answer she had offered on each previous visit: 'I haven't seen my son since he came to see me at work on Friday afternoon, 17 May'. Lodgers at the house, Stanley Sheminant and Irene Dunning, also appeared unaware of the whereabouts of the 19-year-old soldier.

However, they weren't telling the truth. The couple did indeed know the answer to the mystery: Private Beresford had been battered to death with a hammer and Sheminant had buried him beneath the floor in the downstairs front parlour, which they occupied.

There they were to remain until Mrs Berrisford became suspicious. On 17 May, her son had called to see his mother at work, telling her he was going home and would see her later that day. She would never see him again. Stanley Sheminant, off work with a leg injury, told her that Harry had had a drink of tea, and then gone to see a girl before returning to his unit.

The repeated calls by the military police and the unusual smell that was coming from her lodgers' room caused her to take her suspicions further. With her lodgers out of the house, she forced the door and entered the front parlour, noticing that the piano was missing and the carpet had been replaced with an oilcloth. Taking a screwdriver, she returned to the parlour and prising up the floorboards, she made a gruesome discovery. Private Harry Berrisford could now be removed from the list of army deserters.

Sheminant, a 28-year-old bus driver, was detained later that night and at Hanley police station, he claimed that the death had been accidental, that Berrisford had struck his head on the hearth during a fight, and he had panicked, concealing the body beneath the floorboards.

A post-mortem revealed that Berrisford had been battered to death with a hammer and had probably been under the floorboards for two months.

When Sheminant stood trial before Mr Justice Hilbery at Stafford in November, he maintained what he had said at his arrest that the soldier had died accidentally during a struggle. His counsel pleaded guilty to manslaughter but not guilty to murder.

The prosecution disputed this defence and claimed that the accused had committed wilful murder after Berrisford had discovered Sheminant had stolen a number of his belongings while lodging at the house. Fearing being arrested for theft, he had then battered the soldier with a hammer, concealing his body under the floorboards in his room and spending the next two months sleeping in the room with his girlfriend.

Professor James Webster, who had conducted the post-mortem, told the court that the cause of death was from blows to the head and he produced in court the victim's skull to illustrate this. It would have taken considerable violence to shatter the skull, he maintained, effectively dismissing the defence's suggestion that the injuries could have been the result of a heavy fall. The jury took less than thirty minutes to find Sheminant guilty as charged.

The house on Cromwell Street where Stanley Sheminant murdered and concealed the body of Harry Berrisford. (*Author's collection*)

51

'OPERATION FINGERPRINT'

Peter Griffiths, 19 November 1948

The call to Scotland Yard had been made in the early hours of Saturday 15 May 1948. June Anne Devaney, a patient at Blackburn's Queen's Park Hospital, had been found brutally murdered in the grounds and their assistance was required.

June had been admitted ten days earlier, suffering from pneumonia. A month short of her fourth birthday, she had now recovered and was due to be discharged later that day. Nurse Gwendoline Humphries had done her rounds shortly before midnight and June had been sleeping peacefully, but just over an hour later, when Nurse Humphries noticed a draught blowing through the ward, June's cot was found to be empty. Something else that was amiss too: standing at the foot of the cot was a large glass Winchester bottle, used to hold distilled water, and which was kept on a trolley in the ward. A trail of footprints led across the highly polished floor.

A search of the ward and adjacent bathrooms soon escalated into a full search involving the local police and at 3.17 a.m., the young girl's body was found lying face down in the grass, less than 100yd from the ward and close to the perimeter fence.

As detectives from Scotland Yard hurried to Blackburn, the police surgeon discovered that June had been killed with appalling brutality. She had suffered violent injuries caused by a vicious sexual assault, with death occurring as a result of the killer swinging her by her feet and smashing her head against a wall. There were also bruises to her neck and bite marks to her chest. One Scotland Yard detective recorded that the scene of crime photographs were the most horrifying he had ever seen.

A set of fingerprints was found on the Winchester bottle beside the bed. There were well over a dozen sets of prints on the heavy bottle; some fresh, many having been there for weeks, even months. One by one all those with genuine reason to handle the bottle were eliminated, leaving one crisp, clear set of prints, unaccounted for, and belonging, more likely than not to the killer.

The rogue prints from the Winchester bottle didn't match any on file, which suggested that the killer did not have a criminal record. They were clearly those of a younger person and not worn and disfigured as one would expect from an older man, scarred with decades of hard manual work in mills, mines or factories. Therefore, if the killer was young, it was a likely he was a serviceman.

Four days after the murder, Chief Constable Looms, head of Lancashire CID, made a dramatic announcement: every male over the age of sixteen who had been in Blackburn on the night of 14 May was to be fingerprinted. It was a mammoth task and nothing on this scale had been attempted before. Dubbed 'Operation Fingerprint', the Mayor of Blackburn started off the appeal by offering to become the first volunteer, at the same time reassuring everyone that all prints would be destroyed once they had been eliminated.

There were over a 120,000 residents in Blackburn in over 35,000 homes and although many men were still displaced by the armed forces, detectives still had to produce over 46,000 square cards to collect the print samples. Measuring a little over 3in squared, the card was designed to

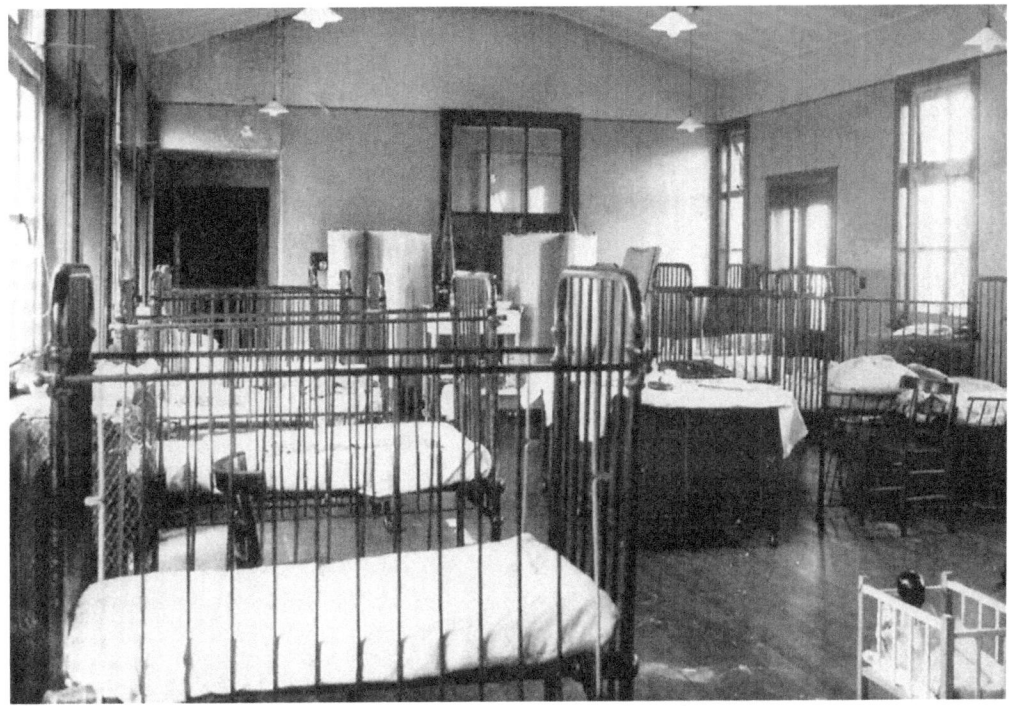

Hospital ward 3B where Peter Griffiths snatched his victim. (*Author's collection*)

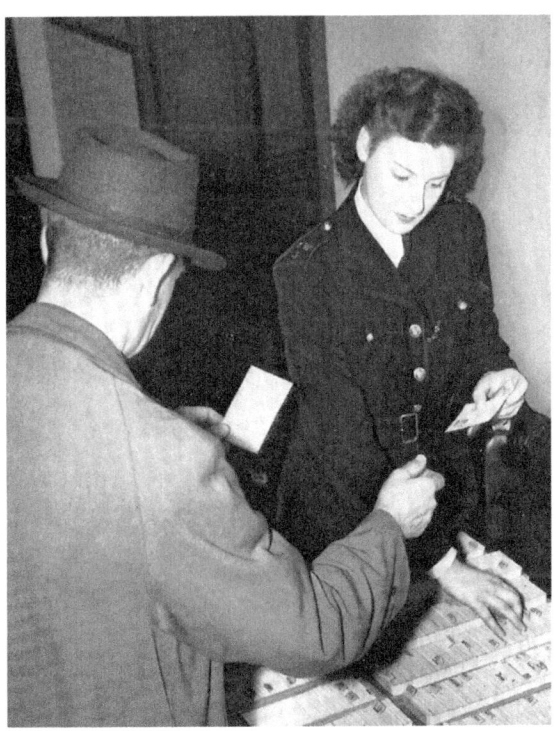

Detectives working on 'Operation Fingerprint'. (Author's collection)

take the impression of the left forefinger and thumb on the front. This would be recorded next to details with the person's name, age, address and national registration number.

By the end of July, with officers working a twelve-hour day collecting and sending prints away for examination, the operation had seemingly ended. All those registered on the Electoral Roll had been accounted for; every print taken had been checked and eliminated. Had the killer slipped through the net?

Then came a breakthrough. At new set of ration books had been issued to returning servicemen, a number of whom were not listed on the registers used in the first checks. Nine hundred names now needed to be checked and this time they got their man. On Thursday 12 August, card number 46235 matched the prints on the bottle.

The card bore the name Peter Griffiths, aged 22, of 31 Birley Street, Blackburn and carried the registration number NBA 6917-188. Griffiths was a tall, ex Welsh-Guardsman who worked in a local mill. He was arrested and under questioning, confessed to the murder: 'If they are my fingerprints on the bottle I will tell you all about it,' he told detectives.

When he stood trial for murder before Mr Justice Oliver on 15 October 1948 at Lancaster Assizes, Griffiths admitted going into the hospital grounds while drunk and trying to make his way home. He had then entered the ward and stumbled against the cot. When the child woke and began to cry, he picked her up to silence her and then carried her outside.

'I walked with her down the hospital field. I put her down on the grass. She started crying again and I tried to stop her . . . she wouldn't stop crying and I just lost my temper, and then you know what happened . . . I banged her head against the wall then went back to put my shoes on . . . I then went back to where the child was. I just glanced at her . . . then went straight down the field . . . '

Above left: Blackburn child-killer Peter Griffiths. (*Author's collection*)

Above right: Griffiths' execution as recorded in assistant hangman Harry Allen's diary. (*Author's collection*)

He said he had then gone home and slept on the sofa and when the story made the front page of the following day's newspaper, he told his parents he had not been anywhere near the hospital.

Faced with the prisoner's confession, his defence chose the only option open to them: to plead that Griffiths was insane. It was claimed that the prisoner had a history of mental illness and that his father had once been an inmate in Prestwich Asylum. His mother testified that as a child Griffiths had fallen off a milk float and had banged his head and from then on, he was prone to blackouts.

The prosecution dismissed any claims of insanity by showing how Griffiths had covered his tracks by lying about his whereabouts and movements on the night of the murder. Agreeing with the prosecution, the three-day trial ended when the jury took just twenty-three minutes to bring in a verdict of guilty. Griffiths stood unmoved as sentence of death was passed on him.

Had his trial been scheduled a month earlier, Griffiths would not have been hanged. Throughout the spring and summer of 1948, all death sentences had been commuted while Parliament debated whether to abolish the death penalty. This suspension had ended by the time Griffiths took his place in the condemned cell.

A fortnight before Griffiths walked to the gallows, hundreds of citizens, police and reporters gathered, in the presence of a newsreel film crew, to destroy 46,000 of the fingerprint cards which were ceremoniously pulped in a Blackburn paper mill. The rest, over 500, were kept as macabre souvenirs.

52

CHANCE MEDLEY

George Semini, 27 January 1949

The antiquated verdict of 'chance medley' was once used in murder cases where the killing was as the result of a brawl, a fight, or sometimes even a duel. In Victorian times it usually meant that death was deemed not to have involved premeditation, but that the killer was still thought to be at fault in some way. It was, however, rarely used; instead, those charged in these types of crimes were usually convicted of manslaughter.

It was an insult that George Semini wasn't about to let go unpunished, but the extremes to which he went were to cost two young men their lives. On Friday 8 October 1948, the Maltese born 24-year-old George Semini, a strong, powerfully built boxer, had been out drinking and dancing with his girlfriend, Marjorie Seabridge, in Newcastle-under-Lyme, Staffordshire. Shortly before 10 p.m., the couple finished their drinks and set off on foot for her house. Their route home took them up Church Street, past the Talbot Hotel, where three men stood outside the adjacent Assembly Dance Hall.

The three were all building labourers from Liverpool who had been working on an extension at the Stafford gasworks. With their contracts at an end and with a pay packet in their pockets, they had left their lodgings in Swynnerton, travelled into Newcastle and were celebrating their last night in the area before returning to Liverpool the following morning.

The Assembly Dance Hall next door to the Talbot Hotel in Church Street, Newastle-under-Lyme, where Joseph Gibbons was stabbed to death. (*Author's collection*)

'Blimey, she's a big girl!' one of the men called out as Semini and his girlfriend walked past. Semini stopped in his tracks and turned around.

'What did you say?' he demanded, walking up to the three men. Frederick Woodyatt, one of the Liverpudlians, laughed in his face and mocked, 'What's it to you?'

'That's my fiancée,' Semini spat angrily and as he spoke, his fist lashed out, knocking Wyatt to the ground. Another of the men, Joseph Gibbons, looked down at his friend lying stunned on the ground and rubbing his bruised jaw.

'Get up and hit him back' he urged Woodyatt. After all, he reasoned, there were three of them – good fighting odds in anyone's book.

The scuffle had brought other people out of the dance hall and one or two of those who had seen what happened knew Semini and his fearsome reputation as a boxer. They rushed to intervene and taking hold of his arm, they ushered him away. Semini, however, was not going to let the matter drop. He shook off the arms restraining him and rushed back at the three men. The fight was as lethal as it was brief. Semini pulled out a knife and turned on 22-year-old Gibbons and the third man, 20-year-old Charles Stanley. Within seconds, Gibbons had slumped to the ground, stabbed once in the heart; Stanley received a wound to his leg, while Woodyatt, who had stumbled groggily to his feet, was stabbed in the shoulder.

By the time police arrived, Semini had fled the scene, but officers soon learned the identity of the killer and he was arrested at a miners' hostel in nearby Knutton. Semini denied committing the murder, and indeed being anywhere near the dance hall or Church Street and claimed never to have carried a knife. He told police that as he was a boxer, he could look after himself with his fists and had no need of a weapon.

A search of his room was to reveal a clue that would eventually lead him to the gallows. A photograph of Semini posing with a wicked looking sheath knife was found in one of the drawers. Resembling Richard Attenborough's portrayal of hoodlum Pinkie in a recently released gangster film *Brighton Rock*, Semini had posed for the picture in the hope that he could get work in the movies, but instead of finding himself on the silver screen, he instead found himself in the dock before Mr Justice Hallett at Stafford Assizes at the end of November, charged with wilful murder.

This photograph of George Semini holding the knife he used to commit a brutal murder ultimately led to his conviction. (*Author's collection*)

The Hilary Law Sittings began to-day.

COURT OF CRIMINAL APPEAL

MURDER APPEAL : DOCTRINE OF CHANCE MEDLEY

REX v. SEMINI

Before the LORD CHIEF JUSTICE, MR. JUSTICE LEWIS, *and* MR. JUSTICE PRITCHARD

The COURT gave its reasons for dismissing, on December 20, 1948, the appeal of George Semini, who was convicted before Mr. Justice Hallett at Stafford Assizes of the murder of Joseph Gibbons.

Mr. Cartwright Sharp, K.C., and Mr. E. Brian Gibbens appeared for the appellant; Mr. Eric Sachs, K.C., and Mr. Norman Carr for the prosecution.

JUDGMENT

The LORD CHIEF JUSTICE, reading the judgment of the Court, said that in the late evening of Friday, October 10, 1948, the appellant was walking with a young woman past a hotel at Newcastle-under-Lyme when one of three men standing there made an observation about her which the appellant resented. The murdered man was one of the three. The appellant went up to the men and knocked one of them down. He admitted that that was the first blow to be struck. From the evidence it appeared reasonably certain that the deceased incited the man who had been knocked down to fight the appel-

Semini's appeal, as recorded in the press. (*Author's collection*)

With eyewitnesses testifying against Semini, he chose a defence almost unheard of in modern times – 'chance medley'. Although outnumbered by the men who had insulted his girl, Semini, by his own admission, admitted striking the first blow, but with the fight escalating from a fist fight, defence counsel realised that self-defence would have been difficult to argue and opted for the little known and long neglected defence of chance medley in the hope of escaping the gallows. When the issue was debated in court, it became clear that while it was possibly the case that there had been provocation and certainly no premeditation in Semini's case, it was ruled both at the trial and in the subsequent court of appeal that a defence of chance medley no longer applied in modern society.

As Semini awaited execution, a campaign for a reprieve was started which had the support of many people, including the Governor of Malta who visited him in prison and pointed out the bravery he had shown during the war. Semini was invalided out of the RAF following an accident which had resulted in head injuries. These injuries and the possible resultant mental disturbance had been the focus of the appeal which had claimed insanity as defence.

Several days before he went to the gallows, Semini received a letter from Gibbons' mother saying that she had forgiven him for murdering her son and hoped he would be reprieved. He wasn't.

53

THE CAMEO CINEMA
MURDERS

George Kelly, 28 March 1950

> 'However much the Cameo murders remain a mystery we regard the circumstances of Kelly and Connolly's trials as a miscarriage of justice which must be deeply regretted.'
>
> (Lord Justice Rix, 11 June 2003)

On the evening of Saturday 19 March 1949, the Cameo Cinema, a small 'fleapit' on Webster Road, Wavertree, Liverpool, was showing the comedy thriller, *Bond Street*. Over 300 customers were watching the action unfold onscreen, while off screen, a drama that would make headlines in the following day's newspaper was being played out.

By 9.15 p.m., cashier Ellen Jackman had counted the takings and had taken them to the manager's office where 39-year-old Leonard Thomas and his 25-year-old assistant, John Catterall, prepared it for banking. Ten minutes later, six shots rang out. Mrs Jackman and cinema fireman, Patrick Griffin, hurried to investigate and came face to face with a masked gunman, his face covered by a scarf and a trilby pulled down over his eyes. 'Get out of the way!' he barked as he went down the spiral staircase and escaped into the night. Thomas lay dead and Catterall, badly wounded, died later that night.

Despite a manhunt across the city that resulted in over 65,000 interviews, with almost 10,000 homes visited, the investigation progressed slowly. Then, out of the blue, fifteen days after the murder, detectives received an anonymous letter from an informant offering a deal. The writer offered to name those involved in exchange for immunity. The deal was accepted by placing a notice in the *Liverpool Echo*. But nothing happened and the trail ran cold.

Another piece of information landed on Inspector Herbert Balmer's desk. Balmer was a hardened officer who was handling the investigation. A man named Donald Johnson, a 22-year-old petty criminal in custody for assault and mugging, offered in exchange for the officer standing bail for him and his brother, to name the killer. Johnson said he had been with a man named Dugan on the night of the murder. They had discussed robbing the cinema and had travelled to Wavertree but when he learned that Dugan planned to use the gun, they had parted at 9.20 p.m. When this lead petered out, Johnson was deemed to be a time waster and was returned to custody.

A few weeks later a prostitute, Jackie Dickson was arrested for shoplifting. She asked to speak to Balmer and offered him a name if he dropped the charges against her. With the deal agreed, officers spoke to Charles Connelly, a 27-year-old former merchant seaman with a record for petty crime. Connelly claimed he had an alibi for the night of the murder.

Dickson then fled the area and with police wishing to interview her further, she was finally tracked down in Manchester in the company of 23-year-old James Northam. Known as

Above left: The Cameo Cinema in the 1950s. (*Liverpool County Record Office*)

Above right: Cinema manager Leonard Thomas. (*T.J. Leech Archive*)

'Stutty' because of a speech impediment, Northam told detectives he had been involved in the planning stage of the robbery along with Jackie Dickson and a 27-year-old labourer and petty criminal, George Kelly. He said that Kelly had committed the murder while Connolly had acted as a lookout.

Although both men strenuously denied the allegations, they were charged with the murders and on 12 January 1950 stood trial before Mr Justice Oliver. The trial made legal history. Kelly was defended by Miss Rose Heilbron, the first time a woman would lead for the defence in a murder case. Both Kelly and Connelly maintained their innocence and the evidence against them was based solely on the testimonies of people with criminal records. After thirteen days though, the jury could not agree and a retrial was ordered.

Before the new trial date, Connelly was 'leaned on' by detectives and told that they would go lenient on him if he admitted to acting as a look out. If he refused, they warned him he would more than likely be hanged. It was a gamble with his life he didn't want to risk and he opted to plead guilty. He was convicted of robbery and received ten years' imprisonment.

While the guilty plea might have saved Connelly's life, it was to prove fatal for Kelly. Although the two men had maintained that they did not know each other, the second jury decided that like Connelly, Kelly was guilty and as his trial had been for murder, he was sentenced to death.

Above left: John Catterall was shot dead at the Cameo Cinema. (*T.J. Leech Archive*)

Above right: George Kelly. (*Author's collection*)

Kelly went to the gallows pleading his innocence. Fifty years later the case was re-examined by the Criminal Case Review Commission. Evidence found in the police files by someone investigating the case for a book discovered a statement made by Donald Johnson to Detective Inspector Balmer in which Johnson admitted his involvement in the murder. If this had been introduced in evidence, it could well have lead to the acquittal of George Kelly, and whether it was deliberately withheld or not, it was deemed enough to warrant the conviction unsafe. On Wednesday 11 June 2003, the appeal court reached their verdict which was reported in the evening papers with the following statement:

> The court of appeal yesterday overturned the conviction of George Kelly. Announcing their decision, the three appeal judges concluded the original verdict was 'unsafe'. The Crown did not attempt to uphold the conviction. During the appeal, the judges heard that a statement given by a prosecution witness, claiming a man called Donald Johnson had confessed to committing the crime had not been disclosed at the original trial. Merseyside Police will not be re-opening the investigation.

54

THE ALIBI

Alfred Burns & Edward Francis Devlin, 25 April 1952

Fifty-two-year-old widow Mrs Beatrice Rimmer had last been seen alive shortly before 10 p.m. on Sunday 19 August 1951, when a neighbour saw her returning home from a visit to her son. On the following day, her son Thomas found her battered to death inside her neat terrace house at 7 Cranborne Road in the Wavertree district of Liverpool.

The attack had all the hallmarks of a housebreaking – the intruder having entered through a broken back kitchen window. Since the death of her husband some years earlier, the widow had become something of a recluse who, according to local rumour, was sitting on a tidy sum, and more than once in the recent past, the house had been the target for would-be thieves.

The Home Office pathologist told detectives, under the command of Detective Chief Superintendent Balmer, that they were looking for two men, as Mrs Rimmer had been attacked with two different weapons. One weapon, sporting a sharp edge, had lacerated her face, while the other, a blunt weapon, believed to be an electric torch, had fractured her skull. She had been subjected to a fearful beating with over fifteen blows struck to her head.

The enquiry led police to George McCloughlin, a young army deserter on remand in Walton Gaol. McCloughlin claimed to know the identities of the killers and told Balmer that just before the murder, he had spoken with a man in 'Bill's' all-night café in Islington, who had told him he had travelled to Liverpool from Manchester to carry out a job. McCloughlin was invited to get involved in the scheme and at a further meeting, the man had introduced him to a friend who was also to take part. McCloughlin's plans were scuppered when, on Friday 17 August, he was picked up as a deserter.

Balmer was told of the planned robbery. A waitress, June Bury, was to call at the house on Cranborne Road and speak to the old lady. She was to detain the woman in conversation long enough for two men to gain entry through the back, ransack the house and force their way out through the now opened front door and run off down the street. June named the men as 21-year-old Alfie Burns and 22-year-old Teddy Devlin. Both lived in Manchester and despite their relative youth, both were seasoned housebreakers with a string of convictions.

June Bury led them to Marie Milne, known as 'Chinese Marie', Burns' sometime girlfriend, who, after reassurances that she would not be implicated, told Balmer that Burns and Devlin had planned to do the job on Cranborne Road and she was to be the look out. She travelled with them that Sunday evening but on arriving at Wavertree, she was told that she wouldn't be needed and she had returned to the city centre. She said that when the two men met up with her later that night, both had seemed in a highly agitated state and Burns had reassured his friend, telling him not to worry about the old lady as 'we'll be well away before long'.

Burns and Devlin were picked up in Manchester on 19 October. Both denied any knowledge of the murder with Devlin telling police: 'I don't know what you are talking about. I've heard nothing about any murder in Liverpool.' When told of the date of the murder, Devlin produced an alibi he was to stick with throughout the subsequent trial: 'I couldn't have been in Liverpool on that night, and I can prove it . . . I was 'screwing a gaff' in Manchester at the time,' he told Balmer.

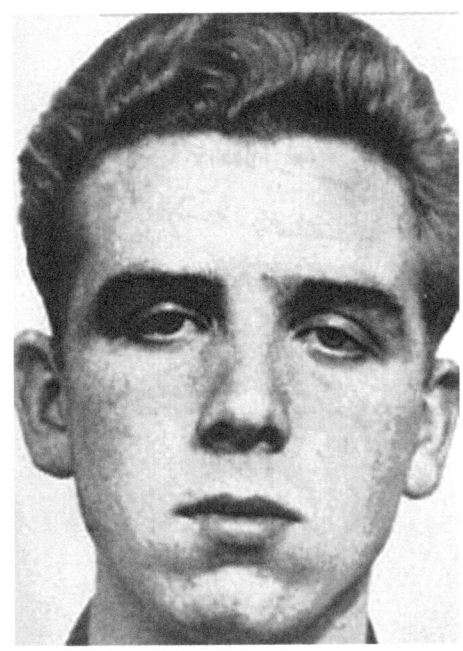

Above left: The house on Cranbourne Road where Alice Rimmer was battered to death. (*Author's collection*)

Above right: Alfie Burns. (*Author's collection*)

Right: Teddy Devlin. (*Author's collection*)

WAVERTREE MURDER TRIAL OPENS

"Blows Rained On Widow"

TWO ACCUSED

Prosecution On Planned Crime

When the trial of two young Manchester men charged with the murder of a Liverpool widow at Wavertree last August opened before Mr. Justice Finnemore and a jury of 12 men at Liverpool Assizes to-day, prosecuting counsel said one of the accused made a knife threat to a girl if she did not take part in a " job " at the widow's house.

Accused are Edward Francis Devlin, aged 22, labourer, of 26 Leinster Street, Hulme, and Alfred Burns, aged 21, labourer of 6 Medlock Street, Deansgate.

A crowded court saw them walk smartly into the dock. Devlin wearing a blue suit and a blue shirt, with a light tie. Burns was also smartly dressed in a lighter blue suit, light blue shirt and blue striped silk tie.

Above: Detective Chief Superintendent Herbert Balmer, who was responsible for sending a number of men, including Burns and Devlin, to the gallows. (*Author's collection*)

Left: Newspaper cutting relating to the Cranbourne Road murder. (*Author's collection*)

Burns, who had been picked up on the day before Devlin as a borstal absconder, also denied any involvement in the murder. His only alibi for that Sunday night in August was that most of the time he had been in the company of Devlin. When presented for identification, a number of witnesses failed to pick them out, but one crucial witness, George McCloughlin, did identify them as the men who had planned to rob the house on Cranborne Road. Although there was blood found on Devlin's suit, he claimed he had recently had a fight and tests linking the blood to the murder scene were inconclusive.

Mr Justice Finnemore presided over the trial at Liverpool Assizes on 19 February 1952. The defence was simple. No one had seen either man enter the house on Cranborne Road, nor commit the murder, and they had an alibi for when it had taken place. They claimed that the prosecution were relying on circumstantial evidence, which both defence counsels planned to refute, along with the testimonies of two girls and a criminal. Both Burns and Devlin seemed oblivious to the seriousness of the charges against them, sniggering at each other and scowling at onlookers in the gallery. The trial progressed slowly until the seventh day when Burns' counsel questioned a young Manchester detective:

'Am I right in saying that on the night of the alleged murder a robbery took place at Sun Blinds Ltd, on Great Jackson Street, Manchester?' The detective confirmed it had. 'What has this to do with the case?' the prosecutor protested. Burns' counsel said that he didn't want to take his learned friend by surprise later and said he planned to prove that Burns could not have been in Liverpool on the night of the murder as he was involved in the aforementioned break-in.

Telephone No. ...Aintree 2228....  H. M. Prison,

All communications should be addressed
to "The Governor" (not to any official by
name), and the following number quoted

Liverpool.

....

Your ref. ....

2nd April, 1952

Sydney Dernley, Esq.,
10, Sherwood Rise,
Mansfield Woodhouse,
MANSFIELD, Notts.

Dear Sir,   No 5736 – E.F. Devlin.

          Will you please note that the execution
of the above-named has now been fixed for 9.0 a.m.
on Friday the 18th April, at this Prison.

          You will be expected to report at this
establishment not later than 4.0 p.m. on Thursday,
17th April, and a railway warrant is enclosed
for your use. Please acknowledge receipt of this
letter.

                              Yours faithfully,

                              Deputy Governor, i/c.

No. 937   (23501–9-11-50)

Letter advising the assistant hangman of the revised date of Devlin's execution.
Following a further appeal, the execution was put back a week. (*Author's collection*)

Newspaper cutting reporting the executions of Burns and Devlin. (*Author's collection*)

Twenty-one year-old Alan Campbell was called to give evidence. He had been convicted of this offence and was currently serving a sentence in Manchester's Strangeways Gaol. Under oath, he now claimed that he had been accompanied on the robbery by both of the accused. Burns and Devlin each took the stand but gave unconvincing accounts of the Manchester robbery. Addressing the jury, the defence counsel said that this alibi corroborated by other witnesses, showed both men were in Manchester on the day of the murder so it was therefore unsafe to convict them.

The prosecution then played their trump card. Challenging the defence, they called Campbell back into the dock to remind him that the offence for which he had been convicted took place on Saturday night, 18 August 1951. This was a full twenty-four hours before Burns and Devlin claimed to have been in the Manchester warehouse. The alibi was destroyed in one fell swoop.

Following conviction and the failure of their appeal, the Home Secretary made legal history by agreeing to launch an inquiry into the investigation. As a result, the execution planned for 18 April 1952 was postponed for a week. On Monday 21 April, the result of the inquiry was published. It claimed that there were no reasonable grounds to suggest a miscarriage of justice had taken place and the law must take its course.

Families of the condemned men wrote frantic letters to the newly ascended Queen Elizabeth to show mercy, but they went unheeded. Campaigners claimed that they were innocent and there had been a miscarriage of justice, but it was reported later that one of the men had made a last-minute confession and this appeared in a Sunday newspaper shortly after the executions.

55

THE OLD CURIOSITY SHOP MURDER

John Lawrence Todd, 19 May 1953

When Iris Tucker came down for breakfast at her home in Park Grove, Bootle, on the morning of Monday 19 January 1953, she little thought that what she read in her morning paper would lead a cold-blooded killer to the gallows.

Twenty-two-year-old Iris worked as a cinema usherette and for the last few days, one of the main topics of conversation among her workmates had been the brutal murder of an old man in nearby Aintree. Sipping her tea, she opened her morning paper and a shiver ran down her spine at what she read.

The paper carried a description of a man wanted in connection with the murder and the detailed description bore an uncanny resemblance to her boyfriend of the last eighteen months. There was also the mention of a bloodstained, fawn raincoat found beside the body – the same colour and type he told Iris he had lost a few days earlier. She called her father who, after reading through the article, telephoned the local police.

Above left: The front window of the Old Curiosity Shop. (*TNA: PRO*)

Above right: The stairway in the Old Curiosity Shop with spots of blood circled with chalk. (*TNA:PRO*)

Right: The body of George Walker found inside the Old Curiosity Shop on Warbreck Moor, Aintree. (*TNA: PRO*)

Later that morning, detectives called at a house in Roxborough Street, Walton, and spoke to 20-year-old labourer, John Todd, who lived there with his mother. It had taken less than a week to solve one of the most brutal murders in post-war England.

Hugh 'George' Walker ran an antique shop at 98 Warbreck Moor, close to Aintree racecourse. Known locally as the Old Curiosity Shop after Dickens' book, it was filled with a myriad of curios, antiques, clocks and electrical goods; it was the sort of place one could browse for hours. Not that Walker encouraged browsers, or even customers; in fact, anyone calling at the shop had to knock loudly and hope they could alert the attention of the 82-year-old proprietor who was slightly deaf.

Walker was a popular old man and neighbours were concerned when, on the night of 14 January 1953, his two mongrel dogs kept the neighbourhood awake with their incessant barking. One neighbour went to investigate but on receiving no answer, assumed the old man had gone to stay with family for the night. On the following day, however, another neighbour began to suspect something was wrong and telephoned the police. When officers forced an entry, they found that something was indeed very wrong. George Walker was lying at the foot of his stairs, bludgeoned and bloodied; beside his battered body lay an axe and in the pools of blood in the hallway were footprints which suggested the killer had worn crepe-soled shoes.

Walker's sister told police that a thin, pale man with a large nose had called to repair some clocks on the previous day and that description matched one given by two schoolboys who had called at the shop on the Tuesday afternoon.

Under questioning, Todd admitted that he had been at the shop on the day of the murder and told an implausible story. He said that he had called there to repair a number of clocks and that the old man had stumbled and fallen against him as he was leaving and had burst his nose in the fall. Walker had then grabbed hold of Todd's coat in an attempt to steady himself, leaving it covered in blood. He had promised to get it cleaned so Todd took off his coat and left it there. He swore that Walker had been alive when he had left the shop and someone else must have gained access later in the day and killed him.

Todd stood trial before Mr Justice Cassels on 8 April 1953. He persisted with his story that the old man had fallen against him and had still been still alive when Todd had left the shop. He could not explain how streaks of blood, consistent with sprays that detectives would expect to find following assault with a weapon such as an axe – known as 'travelling blood' – could have found their way into the lining of his trousers and onto the seam of a jacket he had worn underneath the raincoat.

Iris Tucker gave evidence that when they had met up on the Saturday after the murder and Todd had been without the raincoat, he had told her that the raincoat had been stolen. 'Why, if his version of events was true, did he not tell the truth to his girlfriend?' the Crown asked. Todd was further implicated when he was found to be in possession of certain items of silver that were identified as having belonged to the dead man.

'If you are satisfied that his was the hand that rained those thirty-two savage blows upon the defenceless man's head, then you will find him guilty,' the judge told the jury as he concluded his summing up. The jury took fewer than thirty minutes to find that it was indeed Todd's hand that had dealt the fatal blows.

CURIO-SHOPMURDER: AXE FOUND IN HOUSE

Manchester search

POLICE to-day found a weapon which they think may have been used to murder 82-year-old antique dealer Hugh Walker, whose battered body was found behind the front door of his shop—the Curiosity Shop—near Liverpool's Aintree racecourse.

An attempt had been made to hide the weapon—an axe head with part of the shaft still attached. It was found in Mr. Walker's living quarters above the shop.

Police visited lodging-hou e in Manchester to-day after receiving a description from Liverpool police of a man they wish to interview.

Chief Supt. H. R. Balmer, head of Liverpool C.I.D., said to-day that Mr. Walker was battered

MR. WALKER

Newspaper cutting relating to the Old Curiostiy Shop murder. (*Author's collection*)

John Lawrence Todd. (*T.J. Leech Archive*)

56

UNDER A 'DEFECT OF REASON'

Milton Taylor, 22 June 1954

Milton Taylor and Marie Bradshaw had tried to keep their relationship a secret. As neighbours on Alfred Street, Bury, Lancashire, they had managed to keep their liaisons clandestine until shortly after New Year 1954, when George Bradshaw, Marie's husband of six years, came home early from work and found her in bed with 23-year-old Milton Taylor.

The Bradshaws' relationship, since their marriage in 1948, had been turbulent and although they had two children, the relationship was fraught with problems. Following the discovery of Marie's infidelity, the couple decided to part.

Marie opted to move to Crewe with Taylor and the couple took a room together in a house on Underwood Lane, where, for a time, they seemed happy enough. On Saturday 20 February 1954, Marie's estranged husband, George, visited the flat. His reasons for visiting were twofold: to reconcile their differences and persuade her to return home with him and also to have her act as a character witness in a case brought against him by another woman – for an affiliation order.

The situation was further complicated, however, when Marie revealed to her husband that she was pregnant and that Milton Taylor was the father. Bradshaw agreed to accept the child if they could put the past behind them and start afresh, but the ensuing, sometimes heated discussions drew the attention of the landlady, Mrs Winifred Gregory. Milton and Marie had introduced themselves to her as Mr and Mrs Taylor and now realising their true situation, the landlady told them to pack their belongings and leave. 'I do not want this flat being using for inappropriate liaisons' she told them as they left the house in the company of George Bradshaw.

The three of them walked to Crewe Square from where George Bradshaw returned to Bury, while Taylor and Marie were last seen together at around 10 p.m. that night in a Nantwich snack bar. With little money and no bed for the night, they took shelter in a storage hut in a field on Windy Arbour Farm, Worleston. By the following morning, Marie Bradshaw was dead: a man's necktie was knotted tightly around her neck and her face covered by a red handkerchief, embroidered with grim irony the message, 'Good luck'.

When Milton Taylor stood trial for Marie's murder before Mr Justice Byrne at Chester Assizes on 5 June 1954, the story of how they had become murderer and victim unfolded before a packed assembly.

On Sunday morning, 21 February, Taylor had called on his friend, John Lee Mann, who told the court: 'He came round on the Sunday morning, about 10 am. We exchanged greetings, then he said, "I'm in trouble, John, I've killed Marie". I replied "Oh aye!" thinking he was joking. He then repeated, "I've killed Marie". He was very agitated and as he came across the room to me, he broke down in tears. I calmed him down and asked him why he did it. He said she'd been grumbling about stomach pains and nattering at him. I asked him if he knew what he was doing and he said: "Yes, I meant to kill her". He showed me his hands, which still had blood on them. We decided to go to the police station at Nantwich'.

Right: Marie Bradshaw. (*Author's collection*)

Below: Marie Bradshaw's body as discovered in the hut near Crewe. (*TNA: PRO*

The hut as seen from the road (*above*) and up close (*below*). (*Author's collection*)

Sergeant Thomas Shone, of Nantwich Police told the court how Taylor had come into the station to give himself up and made the following confession: 'I did it this morning. She is in a hut in a field off the Middlewich Road. She would not let me sleep. She got on my nerves, so I strangled her with my tie and covered her face with a headscarf. She lived with me as my wife in Crewe. I did it at about 8.40 a.m. this morning. She got on my nerves in the hut so I strangled her.'

Sergeant Shone added that the accused was not wearing a necktie and that though his hands were dirty, there were no other marks on them.

Taylor's defending counsel questioned the sergeant with regard to Taylor's attitude and demeanour, suggesting that his calm and collected manner, seemingly unaffected by the serious charge against him, showed that he was insane.

There was never any doubt that Milton Taylor had strangled Marie Bradshaw, even though he had offered a plea of not guilty when the proceedings had begun. Dr Isaac Frost, consultant psychiatrist attached to the Deva Hospital, Chester, told the court that throughout his examination of Taylor, the accused had 'smiled in a fatuous and irrelevant way' not appropriate at all for the circumstances he was in. Dr Frost had also conducted various IQ tests with Taylor and concluded that he was feeble-minded, with the mental age of an 11-year-old.

Frost said he had questioned Taylor regarding the murder and was surprised at his reply:

> I strangled somebody, sometime in February. I wanted to. Just felt like it. She didn't upset me. I got satisfaction. Just felt better when I did it with a tie. When I want to do a thing I do it, whatever the consequences. If I felt like it, I would do it to anybody else. I think anybody should strangle anybody if they feel like it. If they feel like it, it would be right from their point of view. The way I look at it, it was right to do it. I don't feel sad or sorry; quite happy as a matter of fact.

Taylor agreed with Dr Frost that other people would think such a thing was wrong and admitted that he knew it was against the law. Dr Frost also added that Taylor had suffered from inflammation of the brain following a vaccination and, in his opinion, Taylor was labouring under a 'defect of reason' and on that February morning did not know the nature of what he was doing or that it was wrong.

In reply, the Crown called Dr Francis Brisby, Principal Medical Officer at Walton Gaol, who testified that he had found no history of mental illness in Taylor's family, nor anything to indicate that Taylor was suffering from mental disorder or inflammation of the brain. They also called Dr McKenzie, Medical Officer at Shrewsbury Prison, to refute the insanity charge. He had also had an opportunity to view Taylor while he was on remand and found that the prisoner knew the nature of his act and that it was wrong. Despite strong evidence that Taylor was suffering from a form of insanity, the jury took just thirty-five minutes to find him guilty of murder.

57

THE BODY IN THE CANAL

William Arthur Salt, 29 March 1955

Saturday 18 December 1954 should have been the day 43-year-old William Salt married his landlady, Annie Shenton, at Hanley, Staffordshire. Instead of walking up the aisle that day, however, Salt found himself in police custody charged with the murder of his fiancée's 6-year-old son, Dennis.

Salt had initially lodged at 62 Cannon Street, Hanley, but soon fell in love with Annie Shenton and, being out of work, would often take her young son to school.

On 16 December, Dennis arrived at St John's School, Birch Terrace, as usual but, shortly before morning break, Salt called at the school and claimed that he needed to take the boy to see his grandmother. Salt was well known to staff at the school and had taken Dennis out of school on other occasions, such as trips to the dentist.

This time was different. At 12.30 p.m. Annie called at the school to collect Dennis and was surprised to discover that her son had been taken out of school. She may have been surprised but was not overly concerned until darkness fell and there was still no sign of either her fiancé

The footpath at Trentham where William Salt threw Dennis Shenton into the canal. (*Author's collection*)

or her son. Shortly after six o'clock, Salt returned home alone, saying he had taken Dennis to his sister in Runcorn. He was a bit vague in his reply as to why he had returned home alone without her son, so Annie suggested they take the train to Runcorn to collect him.

Salt agreed but caused suspicion by disappearing before they could reach the railway station. Annie called the police who soon confirmed that the child was not in Runcorn. Salt was picked up in a nearby public house the following day and admitted drowning Dennis in the canal. He took police officers to a spot on the canal at Trentham where they recovered his body.

Asked why he committed the horrific act, Salt simply said, 'He got on my nerves. We were walking along the towpath hand in hand. The urge came over me and I swung him into the water.'

When Salt was tried before Mr Justice Devlin at Stafford Assizes early in March 1955, his defence sought to show that he was insane. Evidence was heard that Salt had once been injured in an accident in a colliery and had twice suffered head injuries in road accidents, once in 1935, the second eighteen years later in 1953. Since the accidents, Salt had complained of headaches and claimed to be afraid to go out in the dark.

The prosecution refuted the claims of insanity. They maintained that Salt had committed a brutal murder solely because the young lad had done something to irritate him. The fact that he had deliberately taken the child out of school before carrying out the crime showed premeditation but there seemed to be a distinct lack of a motive. It came out at the trial that Salt was already a married man although claims that he may have killed the young boy because he was worried about committing bigamy didn't seem to carry much weight. After considering their verdict for seventy-five minutes, the jury found him guilty of murder.

Salt chose not to appeal against the verdict and was hanged less than three weeks following conviction.

58

'UNTIL THE OTHER ONE CAME'

Richard Gowler, 21 June 1955

In the early hours of Friday 11 March 1955, a telephone call came through to the front desk at Wallasey police station. A woman's voice, frantic with shock, told the sergeant that a man named Gowler had stabbed to death both her mother and sister at their home at 18 Clarence Road, Seacombe, a mile or so from New Brighton. A constable was dispatched to Clarence Road and saw at once that the house had been ransacked: the furniture was overturned, some of it broken, and drawers were pulled out and the contents were strewn across the floor.

Above left: Mary Boothroyd. (*T.J. Leech Archive*)

Above right: Richard Gowler. (*Author's collection*)

Twenty-year-old Margaret Boothroyd, who had put through the emergency call, told the officer that her mother, 53-year-old Mary Catherine Boothroyd, and sister, 26-year-old Dorothy Dearlove, were upstairs. Climbing the stairs, the officer found the body of the older woman lying on the landing. Dressed in her nightgown, she was covered in blood, which was seeping from a large number of deep wounds to her face and upper body. Contrary to what he had been told, the officer found that the woman was still alive, but life was ebbing away by the second. He told Margaret to wait in the road for the ambulance, while he entered the front bedroom where he found the daughter. She had similar injuries to her mother and was also still alive.

An ambulance took the two women to the nearby Victoria Central Hospital at Wallasey. It was a journey of just a matter of minutes, but it was too long for Mrs Boothroyd, who was pronounced dead on arrival. She had been stabbed five times in the chest and three times in the head with a somewhat unusual weapon which resembled a twin-pointed stiletto. The fatal wound had been delivered through the chest and had punctured the large artery close to the heart.

The mystery of what had caused the unusual wounds was soon solved when a detective back at Clarence Road found a bloodstained 20in-long marlinspike. The fearsome looking spike was a common tool at the docks, where it was used to unravel knots in rigging and other strands of rope. It was also the type of instrument usually carried by ships' riggers, which happened to be the occupation of Richard Gowler, the man Margaret Boothroyd had told police was responsible for the attacks.

As doctors fought to save Dorothy Dearlove's life, Gowler was arrested on Magazines Promenade, New Brighton. Officers had been radioed to be on the lookout for Gowler and a description of him was circulated. An officer spotted him acting in a suspicious manner on the pier and spoke to him.'Are you Gowler?' he asked. 'Yes, that's me. You're just in time. I was about to go in off the pier'.

His suicide attempt thwarted, Gowler was placed under arrest and taken to Wallasey police station. 'Are they dead?' he asked when cautioned. When told that Mrs Boothroyd was and that Dorothy wasn't expected to live, he hung his head. 'I am sorry it is the old lady that has gone because I liked her. I lodged with her for a few years and everything was alright until the other one came and caused all the trouble.' Gowler was then formally charged and added to his statement:

> You might as well know the lot. She had me for a sucker and I am mixed up in a divorce case which has upset me. She has had about 300 [pounds] out of me and if you want to know why I went there that night, it was because she had promised three different times this week to see me. She kept me waiting and never turned up.

Detectives and a local magistrate were at Dorothy's bedside when word came through of Gowler's arrest. With thirteen stab wounds to her upper body, including a 4in cut to her liver, little hope was held out for her survival. Detectives gathered by her bedside as in a barely conscious state, she weakly dictated a statement in the form of a sworn affidavit, describing the events which led up to the attack.

Dorothy Dearlove was the mother of a 2-year-old child and had separated from her husband prior to the child's birth in the summer of 1953, moving back in with her mother and sister at Clarence Road. Lodging at the house since 1950 had been 41-year-old seaman, Richard Gowler, a native of West Hartlepool. Dorothy had embarked upon a clandestine sexual liaison with Gowler, which they had kept secret until Mrs Boothroyd found out about it on Boxing Day 1954.

Following a terrific scene, Gowler was told to pack his bags, but he succeeded in pacifying the irate mother and she relented on her decision to evict him on the condition that he ended the relationship with Dorothy. He agreed to the request, but soon began to make endeavours to carry on the affair and as a result, in February 1955, he was again told to leave. This time he took lodgings at a house on Sandrock Road, New Brighton.

Gowler made repeated calls to the house on Clarence Road, but his visits were unwelcome and on more than one occasion, the police were called to rid them of the unwanted caller.

Gowler's murder made the headlines in newspapers across the north-west. (Author's collection)

It was as a result of these nuisance calls that both Mrs Boothroyd and Dorothy took legal advice and a solicitor's letter was sent to Gowler, warning him to stay away. Enraged, he had met up with Dorothy a week before the murder and threatened to kill her if she insisted on avoiding him.

Gowler stood trial at Chester Assizes on Thursday 2 June 1955 before Mr Justice Sellars. Dorothy Dearlove, who had confounded doctors by making a remarkable recovery from her injuries, was present in court, where it was alleged that Gowler had gone to the house with the specific intention of killing Dorothy – only to stand trial for the murder of her mother.

When Gowler took the stand, as the only defence witness, he claimed that he had gone to the house on that fateful night, intending once and for all to speak to Dorothy. He had taken the marlinspike from work intending to use it as a jemmy to force the door, but as it happened, there was a window unfastened and he gained entry that way.

Climbing the stairs, Gowler entered Dorothy's bedroom and touched her face, trying to wake her gently. Instead, she opened her eyes and let out a fearful scream. Gowler claimed that what happened next was a blur, but before he left the house he was aware that both Margaret Boothroyd and Dorothy Dearlove had been seriously wounded. He was particularly upset at seeing Mrs Boothroyd lying at the top of the stairs because at no time did he mean her any harm. His counsel asked the jury to consider a verdict of manslaughter based on the fact that when he had stabbed Mrs Boothroyd, he had had no wilful intention of harming her.

Summing up the evidence, Mr Justice Sellars said that in order for the jury to return a verdict of guilty of murder, they had to be satisfied that 'there had been an intentional and unprovoked killing'.

A little under forty-five minutes later, the jury returned a verdict of guilty of murder and Gowler was sentenced to death.

59

THE WIGAN CHILD MURDERS

Norman William Green, 27 July 1955

For eight months the people of Wigan had been living in fear of the killer striking again. On 27 August 1954, two young boys out playing became the victims of a frenzied knife attack. Seven-year-old Billy Mitchell was cut, but not badly injured; his friend, 11-year-old Billy Harmer, died from his injuries. Mitchell was able to give police a good description of the attacker, but despite a hunt across three counties, police failed to find the killer. Meanwhile, parents took to meeting their children at the school gates and some communities organised a rota of parents to supervise children out playing.

Then, on the night of Easter Monday, 11 April 1955, the killer struck again. Two friends, Jimmy Jones and Walter Wiggins, were listening to the radio in their home on Cross Street in Lower Ince, Wigan, when they heard a scream. Opening the front door, Jones saw that other neighbours had also heard the screams and, lifting the light from Wiggins' bicycle, Jones

Bloodstains on the road show where Norman Yates was stabbed to death. (*Author's collection*)

shouted for his friend and hurried outside. As they reached wasteland at the bottom of the street, they came across a young boy lying, whimpering on the ground. He had been stabbed several times in the head and chest. Identified as 10-year-old Norman Yates, he was rushed to the local hospital where, at 10.20 p.m., he was pronounced dead on arrival.

Norman had left his home on nearby Heywood Street a few minutes earlier to run an errand for his mother, Ivy, and it was clear that he must have encountered his killer almost at once. Detective Chief-Superintendent Cecil Lindsay, who had investigated the first murder hunt the previous August, handled the investigation. Although no one could be found who had seen the killer make his getaway, several witnesses gave police a good description of a man seen in the area shortly before the murder.

On the following evening, Lindsay held a press conference and announced that detectives wished to speak to a man aged around 20–30 years old, between 5ft 2in and 5ft 6ins tall, of slim build with long blonde hair swept back, a sagging jaw – possibly with no teeth – and a prominent nose. It was a description similar to the one issued for the killer of Billy Harmer and from the outset, officers believed that the same man had killed both children.

A post-mortem carried out the next day found that death had been caused by four knife wounds: three to the chest, while the fourth, fatal blow had severed the neck close to the Adam's apple, causing a massive haemorrhage.

Norman Yates was laid to rest on the following Friday afternoon and, as the cortège passed slowly through Lower Ince, the streets were lined with many of his young schoolmates who stood with their caps in their hands, many in tears. As the funeral ended, word spread that a man had been arrested and a large mob converged on Lower Ince police station, where later that night, Lindsay announced that 23-year-old Norman Green, of Hallgate, Wigan, had been charged with the murder of Norman Yates.

 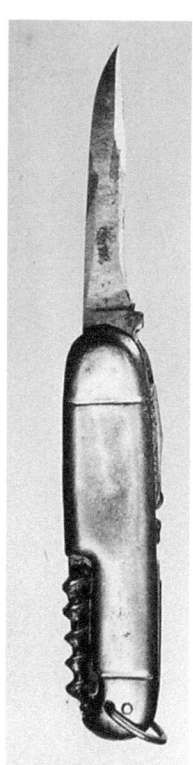

Above left: Norman Green. (*Author's collection*)

Above right: The murder weapon. (*Author's collection*)

Green had been questioned and arrested at his workplace, Charlson and Sons, Corn Millers, on Dawber Street, Wigan, after his name had turned up several times during police enquiries. Two detectives called at the factory shortly after lunch on Friday afternoon and were immediately struck by Green's resemblance to the description of the wanted man.

Asked to account for his movements on the evening of Easter Monday, Green denied having been anywhere near Lower Ince. When detectives told Green they didn't believe his version of that night's events, he altered his story a little, admitting that he had been drinking in the Railway Hotel, Lower Ince. 'I have told you the truth now. I was in the Railway but had nothing to do with that boy,' he said, as he was taken to the station.

One of the detectives went to Green's home and took away the blue suit he had been wearing on Easter Monday. When told it was being sent for examination at the forensic laboratory at Preston, Green broke down and confessed to the murder. 'I am sorry. I am very sorry for his mother. I hope she forgives me for what I have done,' he blurted out, before making a statement describing the attack on Norman Green, but denying any involvement in the other murder from the previous year. Green then accompanied detectives back to his workplace, where he handed over the knife, hidden in a sack.

Officers investigating the murder of William Hamer questioned Green on the following morning. 'Why don't you get it off your chest?' one of them asked him during a break in questioning and, with an air of resignation, Green finally admitted responsibility for the earlier crime.

Above: The Railway Arms, Ince. (*Author's collection*)

Right: Hangman Albert Pierrepoint's last execution was that of Wigan child-killer Norman Green. (*Author's collection*)

Green was committed for trial at the next sitting of the Liverpool Assizes, but with the court due to convene in only a few days' time, his counsel requested the case be put back so that they could prepare his defence. As a result, his case was heard before Mr Justice Oliver at Manchester Assizes in the first week of July.

The defence maintained that Green was insane when he committed the murders and was therefore not responsible for his actions. They claimed that Green had an urge to kill that he couldn't fight. The defence called a number of doctors to support their insanity claims and, as the trial unfolded, it seemed that the insanity plea would sway the jury.

In summing up, the prosecuting counsel dismissed Green's claims of insanity and told the jury that the facts were simple. Green was a wicked child-killer who had murdered two young boys and made a failed attempt to kill a third. They referred to the statement Green had made after his arrest in which he admitted the killing:

> Yes, I killed him. I had been at the Railway Hotel until 9 p.m. when I left by the back door after visiting the lavatory. As I stood at the door I caught sight of a young boy coming down the street. I walked up the entry and the boy followed me. I turned around and asked him where I could get a glass of water. The boy said I could get one at his mother's home and I followed him across the street towards the house. We crossed the back street and I killed him there. When I killed him he screamed. I stabbed him four times.

Summing up, Mr Justice Oliver said that the evidence heard during the trial made it was clear that Green was the killer. The jury were left to decide if he was guilty of wilful murder or insane as the defence claimed. They took just fifteen minutes to find Green guilty as charged.

His appeal was duly dismissed and Norman William Green went to the gallows with the dubious honour of being the last man hanged by long serving executioner, Albert Pierrepoint.

60

THE LAST TO HANG

Peter Anthony Allen, 13 August 1964

It didn't take long for detectives investigating the brutal murder of 53-year-old John West to work out who their prime suspect was. It was in the early hours of Tuesday 7 April 1964 when neighbours heard sounds of a disturbance coming from the house on King's Avenue, Seaton, on the outskirts of Workington. After being woken by a series of heavy thuds, then a scream, followed a short time later by the slamming of a car door and the screeching of tyres, neighbour Joseph Fawcett hurried next door. When he could get no answer to his knocking and shouting through the letter box, he called the police.

Within minutes officers arrived at the house and, after gaining entry with the spare key the neighbour knew was kept in the garden shed, they found the body of John West at the foot of the stairs. He had been battered about the head and was lying partially naked and motionless in a pool of blood.

Above left: The house at 28 King's Avenue, Seaton, Workington. (*Author's collection*)

Above right: Peter Anthony Allen: the last man to hang. (*Author's collection*)

By 4.30 a.m., Detective Inspector John Gibson had begun the murder enquiry. There was no sign of a forced entry, while a search of the house soon yielded valuable clues. On a chair in the bedroom was a neatly folded, modern looking, off-white coloured raincoat. It didn't look like the kind of coat a 53-year-old bachelor would wear, apart from being the wrong size.

One of the officers emptied the pockets and the first item removed was a combined wallet and key holder. Inside the wallet was an army memorandum form filled out with the name Norma O'Brian with an address off Princess Road, Liverpool 8. Attached to the key fob were a number of Yale, locker and car keys, but more importantly, there was also a medal presented by the Royal Life Saving Society in the name of 'G.O. Evans, July, 1961'.

Detectives in Liverpool found that the surname on the memo form had been misspelt, and a Norma O'Brien was interviewed. She recognised the wallet and medal as belonging to Gwynne Owen Evans, a 25-year-old Londoner, whom she knew as 'Ginger', and whom she had met at Fulwood Barracks in Preston. She also gave officers an address in Cumbria where she thought Ginger lived. Officers went to the house at Camerton, three miles from Seaton, but found no one by the name of Evans living there, the occupants being a family called Walby.

It took detectives a while to realise that Ginger Evans' real name was John Robson Walby and, in the meantime, a check through criminal records had given Evans' last address as Clarendon Street, Preston, ninety miles from Seaton. Officers in Preston found the house occupied by a man called Peter Allen, who had turned 21 just a week earlier, and his two young sons. He confirmed that Evans, whom he knew as Sandy, rented a room in his house, and said that the lodger had gone with Mrs Allen to Manchester, where Evans was meeting his girlfriend and Mrs Allen was visiting her parents.

Allen was asked to accompany police to the station to make a statement. He was initially reluctant to leave the children, but once reassured they would be well cared for until his return, he agreed to the request. He kissed his children goodbye and climbed into the police car, little suspecting that he would only see his children just one more time. At the station he gave officers an address in Manchester and Evans was picked up and questioned by officers later that afternoon.

During a search of the wanted man's belongings, an officer felt something concealed in the lining of Evans' jacket. He produced a bunch of keys, but as this was not what the officer had felt, reluctantly, Evans rummaged again in the jacket lining and withdrew a watch inscribed J.A. West. Efforts had been made to obliterate the name, but it was still clearly visible. Mrs Allen was also searched and in her basket was a bloodstained jacket which she admitted belonged to her husband. Both Evans and Allen were taken into custody and interrogated separately.

Meanwhile, a post-mortem revealed that the cause of death had been a fatal stab wound to the heart, but there were also thirteen split wounds to the head caused by a heavy blunt instrument, consistent with the lead pipe found beside the body. No mention of a knife had appeared in any of the newspapers reports and the general impression was that West had been battered to death.

Evans had known the dead man for several years and had once worked with him briefly at the Lakeland Laundry in Workington, where West had worked for over thirty years.

Victim John West.
(*Author's collection*)

Evans maintained that they had remained friends and that West, whom he claimed was a homosexual, had told him many times if he ever needed money, he would give him a loan.

In the spring of 1964, both Allen and Evans owed money in fines and, with Allen faced with a large rates bill, the two decided to travel to Seaton to see West about a loan. On the evening of 6 April, they stole a car from outside a Preston public house and, picking up Allen's wife and children who were going along for the ride, set off towards Cumbria.

According to Evans, he entered the house around 2 a.m. and West agreed to lend him money, but under certain conditions. They went up to the bedroom, where Evans took off his coat and folded it over a chair. He claimed that a short time later, Allen had burst in demanding money and battered West with the heavy cosh they had taken with them, before stabbing him in the heart. At no time did Evans admit using any violence against John West. The mention of the knife was of interest to the police as no one, other than senior detectives and the pathologist, knew that a knife had been used in the murder.

Allen's account varied slightly. He said that Evans had come out of the house and beckoned him inside. Allen said that he went up the stairs, whereupon West came out of the bedroom and, seeing Allen, rushed at him. Allen admitted that he punched him once in the face before going into the bedroom to rummage for money and any bank-books he could find, while Evans carried on attacking their victim on the stairs.

By the time their case came to trial at Manchester Assizes before Mr Justice Ashworth in July, the two friends had become sworn enemies, following a statement Evans made, saying that he had been having an affair with Allen's wife while lodging at the Preston house.

The case against them was simple. They needed money and had gone to the house in Seaton with the intention of stealing and, during the robbery, John West was fatally wounded.

Hangman Robert Leslie 'Jock' Stewart carried out the last execution at Liverpool. (*Author's collection*)

Both blamed the other for striking the fatal blow, but in the end, both were deemed equally responsible and were found guilty as charged.

Since 1957, a new law had been in existence which categorised murder into two strands. Murder during the furtherance of theft was now deemed to be capital murder and carried the death penalty. Consequently, following conviction, Mr Justice Ashworth sentenced both men to death.

Evans was taken to Manchester's Strangeways Prison, while Allen was taken to Walton. They were scheduled to hang at the same time, 8 a.m. on Thursday 13 August. Five days before the execution was due to take place, Allen was visited by his wife and young sons on the youngest boy's first birthday. This was the last time he saw his children. On Wednesday 12 August, a few hours before he was to go the gallows, Allen had his final meeting with his wife. Separated from her by a large partition of bulletproof glass, Allen lost his composure as the meeting came to an end, throwing himself at the glass, causing it to crack and breaking his thumb in the process.

On the following morning, as hangmen Jock Stewart and Harry Robinson entered the condemned cell, Allen was sporting a large bandage around his hand. As they led him onto the drop, he suddenly shouted out, 'Jesus!' Moments later, the last man to be hanged at Liverpool paid the ultimate penalty, while, across the county, his partner in crime met the same ignominious ending on the gallows.

Hanging was suspended the following year and officially abolished in 1969. They were not to know it at the time, but the names of Allen and Evans would pass into criminal history. They were the last to hang.

UNDER SHERIFF'S OFFICE
21 CASTLE STREET
CARLISLE

GLSL

Dear Sir,   14th July 1964

      re: 11115 Peter Anthony Allen

      The above is a prisoner at H. M. Prison, Liverpool, who was sentenced to death on 7th July for Capital Murder.

      By reason of the fact that the offence took place in Cumberland the High Sheriff of this County is charged with the duty of making arrangements to carry out the sentence.

      The prisoner has made an application for leave to Appeal which application, I understand, will be heard on Monday 20th July next.

      In the event of the sentence being carried out I shall be glad if you will let me know if you will undertake the duties. In view of the application for leave to Appeal, no date has yet been fixed.

      I enclose a stamped addressed envelope for your reply.

R. L. Stewart, Esq.,   Yours faithfully,
2 Birchenlea Street,
CHADDERTON,
Lancs.

Letter requesting Stewart's services at Walton. (*Author's collection*)

APPENDIX I

Date of Execution	Convict (age) Executioner(s)	Crime
24 August 1835	James Barlow (42) William Calcraft*	Murdered his wife at Bury
11 April 1836	Elizabeth Rowland (46) William Calcraft*	Murdered her husband at Manchester
21 April 1838	Edward Hill (27) William Calcraft*	Rape and murder at Warrington
3 September 1842	Francis Bradley (32) William Calcraft*	Murdered his wife at Manchester
6 May 1843	Wilmot Buckley (22) Elizabeth Eccles (38) William Calcraft	Murdered his wife at St Helens Murdered her stepson at Bolton
20 January 1844	John Roberts (27) William Calcraft	Murdered a gamekeeper at Knowsley
4 January 1845	George Evans (22) Thomas Stew (21) William Calcraft	Murdered his girlfriend at Manchester Murdered his girlfriend at Manchester
16 September 1848	William Adams (32) William Calcraft	Murdered his wife at Manchester
6 January 1849	James Kelly (24) William Calcraft	Murder of a woman at Stockport
15 September 1849	John Wilson Gleeson 926) Nathaniel Howard	Murder of a family at Liverpool
26 April 1851	Patrick Lyons (21) William Calcraft*	Murder at Warrington
3 January 1856	Jonathan Heywood (47) William Calcraft	Murder at Rochdale
11 September 1857	Henry Rogers (37) William Calcraft	Murder on the high seas
1 January 1859	Henry Reid (40) William Calcraft	Murder at Manchester
8 September 1860	Thomas Gallagher (40) William Calcraft	Murder of his wife at Liverpool
11 January 1862	Patrick McCaffery (29) William Calcraft	Murder of two soldiers at Preston

13 September 1862	William Robert Taylor (37) John Ward (30) William Calcraft	Murdered a man Murder of a policeman in Manchester
3 January 1863	Thomas Edwards (32) William Calcraft	Murder at Liverpool
25 April 1863	Duncan McPhail (34) William Calcraft	Murdered a woman at Blackburn
12 September 1863	George Woods (35) John Hughes (51) James O'Brien (26) Jose Maria Alvarez (22) Ben Thomas (24) William Calcraft	Murdered a man Murdered his wife Murdered a woman Murdered a man Murdered a woman
9 January 1864	William Luke Charles (29) William Calcraft	Murdered his wife at Bury
16 April 1864	James Clitheroe (22) William Calcraft	Murdered a school mistress at St Helens
7 January 1865	Henry Brown (32) William Calcraft*	Murdered a man at Liverpool
1 September 1866	Thomas Grimes (30) William Calcraft	Murdered a colliery worker at Wigan
14 September 1867	Henry Farrington (25) William Calcraft	Murdered his wife

* Unconfirmed but probable

APPENDIX II

Private Executions at Kirkdale House of Correction 1870–1891

Date of Execution	*Convict (age)* *Executioner(s)*	*Crime*
10 January 1870	John Gregson (27) William Calcraft	Murdered his wife at Wigan
8 January 1873	Richard Spencer (60) William Calcraft	Murdered his wife at Liverpool
8 September 1873	James O'Connor (29) William Calcraft & William	Murdered a man in Liverpool Marwood
5 January 1874	Thomas Corrigan (23) Robert Anderson	Murdered his mother at Liverpool
31 August 1874	Henry Flanagan (22) (8 a.m.) Mary Williams (40) (9 a.m.) William Marwood	Murdered his aunt at Liverpool Murdered a man at Bootle

4 January 1875	John McGrave (20)	Murdered Richard Morgan in Liverpool
	Michael Mullen (17)	Murdered Richard Morgan in Liverpool
	William Worthington	Murdered his wife at Wigan
	Robert Anderson	
19 April 1875	Alfred Thomas Heap (41)	Murdered a woman in Manchester
	William Marwood	
6 September 1875	William Baker (35)	Murdered a pub landlord in Liverpool
	William Marwood	
14 August 1876	William Fish (26)	Murdered a young girl in Blackburn
	Richard Thompson (22)	Murdered a man
	William Marwood	
21 August 1877	John Golding (25)	Murdered a man at Edge Hill
	Patrick McGovern	Murdered a man in Liverpool
	William Marwood	
12 February 1878	James Trickett (42)	Murdered his wife in Liverpool
	William Marwood	
28 May 1879	Thomas Johnson (20)	Murdered his girlfriend in Liverpool
	William Marwood	
2 March 1880	Hugh Burns (30)	Murdered their landlord at Widnes
	Patrick Kearns (21)	
	William Marwood	
31 May 1881	Joseph McEntire (42)	Murdered his wife
	William Marwood	
21 August 1882	William Turner (52)	Murdered his wife at Skelmesdale
	William Marwood	
4 December 1882	Bernard Mullarkey (19)	Murdered a man at Maghull
	William Marwood	
3 December 1883	Henry Dutton (22)	Murdered a grandmother at Liverpool
	Bartholomew Binns	
3 March 1884	Catherine Flanagan (55)	Murdered Thomas Higgins
	Margaret Higgins (41)	Murdered her husband, Thomas Higgins
	Bartholomew Binns & Samuel Heath	
10 March 1884	Michael McLean (18)	Murdered a sailor at Liverpool docks
	Bartholomew Binns & Samuel Heath	
19 August 1884	Peter Cassidy (54)	Murdered his wife at Bootle
	James Berry	
8 December 1884	Ernest Ewerstadt (23)	Murdered his former girlfriend
	Arthur Shaw (31)	Murdered his wife in Manchester
	James Berry & Mr Speight	
9 December 1885	George Thomas (29)	Murdered a woman in Toxteth
	James Berry	
15 April 1890	William Chadwick (23)	Murdered a shopkeeper in Atherton
	James Berry	
30 December 1890	Thomas McDonald (32)	Murdered a schoolteacher in Bolton
	James Berry	
20 August 1891	John Conway (62)	Murdered a young boy in Liverpool
	James Berry	

APPENDIX III

Date	Convict	Executioner	Assistant (s)
14 March 1887	Elizabeth Berry	James Berry	
17 August 1892	Patrick Gibbons	James Billington	
3 January 1893	Cross Duckworth	James Billington	
2 April 1894	Margaret Walber	James Billington	Thomas Scott
22 May 1894	John Langford	James Billington	
4 June 1895	William Miller	James Billington	William Warbrick
17 December 1895	Elijah Winstanley	James Billington	Thomas Scott*
18 August 1897	Thomas Lloyd	James Billington	Thomas Billington
27 December 1900	James Joseph Bergin	James Billington	William Billington
24 December 1901	John Harrison	William Billington	Thomas Billington
20 May 1902	Thomas Marsland	William Billington	John Billington
2 June 1903§	Gustav Rau Wilhelm Schmidt	William Billington	John Billington
29 December 1903	Henry Bertram Starr	William Billington	Henry Pierrepoint
31 May 1904+	William Kirwan Ping Lun	William Billington	Henry Pierrepoint
7 August 1907	Charles Patterson	Henry Pierrepoint	Thomas Pierrepoint
30 March 1909	See Lee	Henry Pierrepoint	Thomas Pierrepoint
22 November 1910	Henry Thompson	John Ellis	William Willis
9 May 1911	Thomas Seymour	John Ellis	Thomas Pierrepoint
6 December 1911	Michael Fagan	John Ellis	William Willis
15 December 1911	Joseph Fletcher	John Ellis	George Brown
26 February 1914	George Ball	John Ellis	William Willis
14 May 1914	Joseph Spooner	John Ellis	William Willis
1 December 1915+	John James Thornley Young Hill	John Ellis	William Willis
16 August 1917	William Thomas Hodgson	John Ellis	Edward Taylor
22 July 1919	John Crossland	John Ellis	Robert Baxter
11 May 1920+	Herbert E. L. Salisbury William Waddington	John Ellis	Robert Baxter Edward Taylor
11 August 1920	James Ellor	John Ellis	Edward Taylor

10 April 1923	Frederick George Wood	John Ellis	Thomas Phillips
5 August 1925	James Winstanley	William Willis	Robert Wilson
23 March 1926	Lock Ah Tam	William Willis	Henry Pollard
26 November 1926	James Leah	Thomas Pierrepoint	Lionel Mann
6 December 1927	William Meynell Robertson	Thomas Pierrepoint	Thomas Phillips
25 July 1928	Albert George Absalom	Thomas Pierrepoint	Henry Pollard
12 March 1929	Joseph Reginald V. Clarke	Thomas Pierrepoint	Henry Pollard
26 November 1929	John Maguire	Thomas Pierrepoint	Thomas Phillips
20 June 1933	Richard Hetherington	Thomas Pierrepoint	Albert Pierrepoint
8 June 1938	Jan Mohamed	Thomas Pierrepoint	Albert Pierrepoint
9 April 1941	Samuel Morgan	Thomas Pierrepoint	Herbert Morris
25 March 1942	David Roger Williams	Thomas Pierrepoint	Stephen Wade
24 June 1942	Douglas Edmondson	Thomas Pierrepoint	Herbert Morris
10 February 1943	Ronald Roberts	Thomas Pierrepoint	Harry Kirk
29 December 1943	Thomas James	Thomas Pierrepoint	Herbert Morris
12 July 1944	John Gordon Davidson	Thomas Pierrepoint	Alex Riley
17 July 1946	Thomas Hendren	Albert Pierrepoint	Herbert Morris
7 August 1946	Walter Clayton	Albert Pierrepoint	Stephen Wade
19 November 1946	Arthur Rushton	Albert Pierrepoint	Henry Critchell
3 January 1947	Stanley Sheminant	Stephen Wade	Harry B. Allen
19 November 1948	Peter Griffiths	Albert Pierrepoint	Harry B. Allen
27 January 1949	George Semini	Albert Pierrepoint	Harry B. Allen
28 March 1950	George Kelly	Albert Pierrepoint	Harry B. Allen
25 April 1952§	Alfred Burns Edward Francis Devlin	Albert Pierrepoint	Syd Dernley Harry Smith Robert L. Stewart
19 May 1953	John Lawrence Todd	Albert Pierrepoint	Joseph Broadbent
22 June 1954	Milton Taylor	Albert Pierrepoint	Robert L. Stewart
29 March 1955	William Arthur Salt	Stephen Wade	Harry Smith
21 June 1955	Richard Gowler	Albert Pierrepoint	Robert L. Stewart
27 July 1955	Norman William Green	Albert Pierrepoint	Robert L. Stewart
13 August 1964	Peter Anthony Allen	Robert L. Stewart	Harry Robinson

§ signify a double execution

+signify double executions of killers not connected and hanged for separate crimes

* Scott was engaged but was not present at the execution (see Introduction)

INDEX